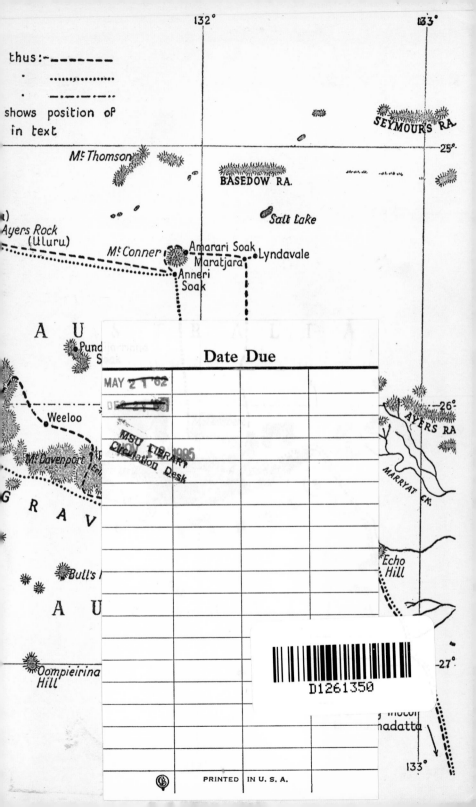

BROWN MEN AND RED SAND

BROWN MEN
AND RED SAND

JOURNEYINGS IN WILD AUSTRALIA

Charles P. Mountford
F.R.A.I., F.R.G.S, Etc.

FREDERICK A. PRAEGER
NEW YORK

Published in the United States
in 1952 by Frederick A. Praeger, Inc.,
Publishers, 105 West 40th Street,
New York 18, N.Y.

919.4
M864b

'BOOKS THAT MATTER'

Dedication

To my parents, who taught me to appreciate the strange and the beautiful.

To my wife, whose help and co-operation have been a constant stimulus.

To the brown people, for their patience and forbearance.

foreword

In 'brown men and red sand'
we have an authoritative account of the aboriginal inhabitants
of Central Australia by one who knows them intimately,
and knowing them must needs love them. I was privileged
to be accompanied by the author when he made his first visit
into Central Australia and I shall never forget the grandeur
of the scene when our small party arrived under the shadow
of a 'great rock in a weary land,' Ayers Rock, as Tietkens the
explorer, quoting Scripture, described its companion, Mt.
Olga. During that journey I became acquainted with three
aspects of Mr. Mountford's interests and activities. One
was his love for the artistic, and anyone who has seen his
photography will recognize in it a master's hand. And, in
truth, the natural features of the Inland—the smooth,
white-dusted stems of the ghost gums rising from the midst
of the rocks, the quaint and distorted trunks of the corkwood
trees, the pendant branches of the ironwood, the native
cypress pines on the hill-slopes, the desert Casuarina oaks
under whose welcome shade one may rest during the noon-
day spell, the rich deep red of the sand-ridges whose crests
support that quaint tree-like shrub that rejoices in the name
of *Gyrostemon ramulosus,* the sunsets of the most lovely
tints of pink and red and yellow deepening into indigo as
the arc of night overtakes the day, the tumbled masses of
rock, the great ravines, the dome of Ayers Rock, the minarets
of Mt. Olga, the poise of the men, the graceful forms of
the native children, the stars at night in bewildering brilliance, some flashing alternately red and blue—all these
features and many more demand an artist's skill to limn
them and the words of a poet to sing their praise.

Another of Mr. Mountford's activities was shown by his
taking every possible opportunity of collecting the folk-lore
of the aborigines, visiting their ancestral sacred places and
studying all sides of their daily life.

And thirdly, and most important of all, there was his evident love and affection for them, a regard that made him indignant over their neglect at the hands of many who were indeed indebted to them for many services, and furious at the ill-treatment sometimes accorded them by thoughtless or undesirable white people.

Though many have written accounts of our Australian aborigines and the country they inhabit, these are mostly either scientific treatises, often of great anthropological value, or popular descriptions where accuracy of detail has suffered through the inexperience of the writer. *Brown Men and Red Sand* not only holds the attention of the general reader but is also a storehouse of reliable information of anthropological value on the legends and daily life of our natives of the interior. With admirable skill, the author has interwoven, in the general account of his journey to the Musgrave Ranges and western Central Australia, the native legends of the natural features of the regions that he traversed. The aborigines are keen observers and have in full degree that human quality of inquisitiveness. Here are rocks, or a waterhole, the bed of a salt lake or a constellation of stars in the sky. How came they to exist? Not surely just by happy chance. Something must have happened to produce them, just as in the daily search for food or maybe water or in the holding of a sacred ceremony the men of today do things and leave behind traces of what they did. What more natural, what more learned than for the aborigines to ascribe to ancestral beings the capacity to do things on a grander scale than themselves and to devise in detail how those great works had been done? We ourselves have only recently emerged into an age of more exact knowledge from one in which natural objects were seen through an anthropomorphic screen.

Mr. Mountford's journey is one of many that has helped to make the history of Australia. As you follow his party on their course you will feel with him the anxieties that he experienced; you will realize as he did the dangers of being cut off from return by the drying up of rock-holes supposed to be permanent; you will rejoice with him when, against all reason, the native medicine-men brought delightful showers on that thirsty land that enabled further exploration to be carried out; and you will sense that feeling of goodwill, law-abidance and humour and even a little of the vanity that go to make up one of the most lovable of the races of mankind, our Australian aboriginal.

J. B. CLELAND, M.B., CH.M., F.R.A.C.P.,
Chairman, Board of Anthropological Research.

University of Adelaide,
  January 1st, 1948.

Contents

List of Illustrations

Introduction

THIS BOOK IS NOT AN anthropological treatise; it is the story of my journey among the desert aborigines of Central Australia and of the experiences that I shared with them. From the standpoint of the scientist, the story of their life is by no means completed by this book; much more research has to be carried out before the gaps can be filled.

It may be contended by some that I have painted an idealistic picture of the aboriginal people. Perhaps I have, but my impressions were based on the study of their culture, their relationship to each other, and the many courtesies and help that we received at their hands. It was an unforgettable experience to have lived among a people whose laws were so kindly and well-balanced that there is no need of warfare to maintain social equilibrium.

In the carrying out of the research and the writing of this book, I have been helped by many. The first tribute is to my young companion, Lauri, for his unobtrusive help and companionship; to his father, Mr. H. L. Sheard, to Miss E. M. Symon, and to Mrs. M. Clark for their generous donations toward the expedition funds; to Professor J. B. Cleland, whose quiet support I have always appreciated; to the staff of the Ernabella Mission Station, for their help; to the Commonwealth Literary Fund, whose grant made the writing of this book possible; to Dr. and Mrs. E. G. Biaggini for their unstinting help in the correction of the manuscript; and to my wife, for her stern and unbending attitude toward my literary misdemeanours.

CHARLES P. MOUNTFORD.

St. Peters,
    South Australia.
        1st January, 1948.

CHAPTER I

The Departure

THE GREAT MOMENT HAD arrived! For years I had hoped and planned to live among the aborigines of the western deserts of Central Australia so that I could study their art, their legends and their social customs, and now, after weeks of preparation, we were off.

The 13th of the month, what a date! Yet, when we set out on the bright June morning, we did not even remember the ancient superstition.

The party was small: my wife ('Johnnie'), Mr. L. E. Sheard (Lauri), and myself. My wife accompanied us with some misgiving. Previously she had sought the green places of the earth, mountain ranges clouded with mist, or fern-tree gullies dripping with the spray of waterfalls. Now she was going to a country where it seldom rained; instead of cloud-encircled mountains and graceful ferns there would be red sunburnt rocks, and gaunt desert trees. I knew that she would see the charm of those rough, barren hills, and the plains that sweep away to infinity, even though the appreciation of the new beauty might take time. Once realized, however, it would be no less absorbing than the old.

With Lauri it was different. He was young, and youth loves adventure and change. What cared he if the surroundings were unlike those that he knew? To see, to know, to conquer, was life to him.

We journeyed north from Adelaide through agricultural lands, chequered with paddocks chocolate-brown from the newly-turned soil, or tinged with the faintest green by the tiny leaves of the wheat lately sprung to life. It was midday when we reached Port Pirie, a town built on a swamp that has neither been fully covered nor conquered, and with extensive silver-lead works that contribute largely, if not

1

exclusively, to both the wealth and the dinginess of the place.

From Port Pirie to Port Augusta the railway line skirts the low swampy flats which are, in reality, the eastern shores of Spencer's Gulf. These flats provide a sharp contrast to the rocky walls of the Flinders Ranges, which rise abruptly from the plain to over a thousand feet. The ranges are always attractive. Every time I pass, I watch the changing lights and shades on their deeply furrowed slopes, and forget the waste of swamps and sandhills on the other side.

At Port Augusta we wandered aimlessly round the town for about three hours, while tons of mail, luggage and supplies were moved by hand to the narrow-gauge train that was to take us to Central Australia.

We left about sunset, and, as the engine puffed and struggled up the steep, sinuous track that leads through the Pitchi-Richi Pass, we caught glimpses of white-trunked eucalypts, curiously distorted grass-trees, and, behind them, the pyramidal form of the Devil's Peak, all flooded with the golden radiance of the setting sun.

It was unfortunate that we passed the northern Flinders Ranges at night, as they are by far the most beautiful part of the journey to Central Australia. For almost two hundred miles the train either meanders through the low foothills or skirts the precipitous western face of the ranges. In the daylight one can feast one's eyes on the rugged outlines of the hills, and the colouring of rocky precipices, or even the purples of distance. The most spectacular scenery of the journey lies between Merna-Merna, at the western end of Wilpena Pound, and Parachilna. From there onwards the hills decrease in height, until at Marree, which we reached on the second day of our journey, the plains of the Lake Eyre basin are quite level.

The Lake Eyre basin, the driest and most barren region in Australia, was once a part of a great inland sea which extended from the Gulf of Carpentaria to Marree. The forests which grew along its shores sheltered wombats the size of elephants, as well as giant kangaroos and emus, and in the water swarmed crocodiles and other sea creatures. Later geological movements caused the sea to retreat, and the country to become progressively arid, until today there are few places in the world more desolate and inhospitable. The land and sea creatures perished long ago, and all that we have learned about them has been gathered from the examination of their fossil remains, and the dim stories of the aboriginal myths. At the present time that once well-watered land receives a rainfall of less than five inches a year, so that it is a country of dry watercourses, sunbaked plains, sparse, stunted vegetation and shimmering mirages.

Lying in the centre of this barren wilderness is Lake Eyre, three thousand five hundred square miles in area, and forty feet below sea level, even at the margins. Although the Lake is the central point of a huge drainage system, considerably larger in extent than the whole of New South Wales, so much of the water is absorbed in the surrounding deserts that little of it reaches the thirsty surface. Even when it does, with an evaporation rate of a hundred inches a year the water soon dries up. The Lake Eyre basin has been called 'The Dead Heart of Australia,' and the train journey through that inhospitable region leaves no doubt as to the aptness of the term. But one must fly over its red, arid deserts and stony plains fully to realize its terrifying desolation.

Yet so strange are the ways of nature, that, beneath that burning wilderness, lie the inexhaustible waters of the Great Artesian Basin. Along the south-western edge of Lake Eyre the waters escape to the surface through fissures in the rock, and form another remarkable natural feature, the mound springs. The water of the springs, coming as it does from great depths, is warm and heavily charged with gas and mineral salts, which, deposited by ages of evaporation, aided by drifting sand, have encircled many of the springs with crater-like mounds, some of them a hundred feet in height. Although during the whole of the second day the train passes along the line of the mound-springs, the only one that can be seen is at the Coward Springs railway station.

From that spring a million gallons flow daily to be lost in the sandy desert, for its enclosing mound has been destroyed to allow the stock to water. However, a few miles from Coward Springs there are several remarkable mounds, including the Blanche Cup, the most symmetrical of them, and the Bubbler, from the centre of which a large brown gas-filled bubble periodically rises to the surface.

Marree, on the southern edge of the Lake Eyre basin, is an interesting town. On the eastern side of the railway line are the houses of the white folk, the hotel, the stores, and the post office. On the other side is Afghan town with its galvanized-iron buildings and, well back from the influence of the infidels, a mosque, forbidden to all but the followers of the Prophet. In Afghan town only dignified white-turbanned Asiatics, ill-clad aborigines and strings of camels walk the sandy streets, for in Marree

'East is East, and West is West,
And never the twain shall meet,'

except at the stores, or when the mail is being delivered through the absurdly small windows of the local post office.

The country north of Marree is surprisingly empty. At most of the railway sidings the only signs that they are places where passengers arrive and depart are a small box, two notice boards, on one of which a tattered time-table is posted, and a long destination board, bolted to two uprights, with the name of the siding on it.

At Curdamurka officialdom has achieved a masterpiece. The station, which consists of no more than the usual box and notice board, lies in the middle of a level plain, which extends without break to the horizon. I could see the dust of a motor car five miles away. Yet ahead of where the weekly engines come to rest were two notices, one on either side of the line, warning all and sundry to 'Look Out for the Train.'

It was on the second day that we first saw the aborigines, standing back in little groups, either minding the horses and the goods of the station-owners or watching the activities of

(a) A station on the Central Railway line. *(Page 4.)*
(b) "At Curdamurka officialdom has achieved a masterpiece . . . ." *(Page 4.)*

"At William Creek we made the acquaintance of an aboriginal boy called David . . . ."
(Page 5.)

the white folk. The natives work on the outlying stations as drovers, musterers or shearers, for above all things in settled life it is in the handling of animals that the aborigines are most expert.

At William Creek we made the acquaintance of an aboriginal boy called David. A kindly wife of a station-owner had fitted him out for his journey to the railway, but, having no clothes for a boy of twelve, she had used those belonging to a man. The lad, however, was quite unaware of his badly fitting clothes, even though the shirt could have accommodated two of his size, and the hat, but for his ears, would have fallen over his eyes and blinded him.

From Marree onwards the spirit of the Outback crept over the train, its crew, and its passengers. Although one may have become annoyed with the nonchalance of the railway officials in the more southerly stations, that irritation ceased to exist after the first day's travel was over. The stops at each station were so long that one was puzzled how the railway men filled in so much time. Nevertheless, while the train crew and the fettlers, who maintain the lonely line, exchanged news and gossip, the passengers fraternized, and long before the second day had passed knew each other so well that it was only at bedtime they sorted themselves into first and second class travellers.

Our train was a mixed, that is, it carried both passengers and goods, for the railway transported everything that went into the Centre. The vans were loaded with food, vegetables and sheep for the fettlers, and behind them were lines of empty trucks, which, on their return journey, would be loaded to bursting point with stamping, bewildered cattle for the Adelaide markets.

In one of the cattle-trucks were four hens, a small family for so large a compartment. The fun of the day started when a fettler, not knowing the truck was occupied, opened the door. In a flash the family escaped. Everyone on the train, rotund engine-driver, guard, passengers, and even one serious-minded professor, ran after those cackling old hens. They perched under the carriages, flew into the sleeping compartments, or careered across the plain, followed by a line of panting men. I chased one of them until I had no breath left. When I finally sank exhausted in the sand, she was still in top speed, wings out, her feet throwing up little spurts of sand as she fled from the villain who pursued her.

It was midnight when we reached Oodnadatta, the end of our railway journey. The train, as usual, was late, but only two hours. There was an occasion when the train was on time. But that is history, and the reason has not been made public. Still, what are two hours in that country? The bushmen, and I think the railway men too, have adopted the same philosophy as the Chinese. 'Every day brings us nearer to the grave, so why hurry there?'

The town, on inspection next morning, proved to be a straggling settlement on a perfectly level gibber plain. It was certainly unattractive, and not the place where one would stay from choice. Yet the wife of a missionary once told me that the heat mirage on the gibber plain, which she had been able to see from her back door at Oodnadatta, was as beautiful as anything she could remember. So who can say that one place is more pleasing than another? For 'Johnnie' the green-clad valleys; for the missionary's wife the shimmering mirage of the gibber plains on a blazing hot day.

I had had my first initiation into the gibbers not far from Oodnadatta. True, I had passed over small patches, a few miles in extent, on previous Central Australian journeys, but they were as nothing compared with the extensive areas out from Oodnadatta, where literally hundreds of square miles of level, arid plains are blanketed with untold millions of stones. In some places the stones are the size of large boulders, so large that it is impossible to travel over them by motor; in other places the stones, being smaller, fit into each other like a mosaic pavement, and are so tightly packed that even a steel-tired vehicle does not leave a mark. Centuries of exposure to an arid environment and wind-driven sand have so polished those stones that, when looking against the light, the reflection from their myriad surfaces is similar to that from a pool of water.

The origin of the gibber plains is interesting. Millions of years ago, the surface of the flat-topped hills that are now scattered over the plains was the bottom of the sea. Later geological movements lifted the sea bottom several hundred feet. In the millenniums that followed, wind and water erosion have worn down the old sea floor, until all that remain are the flat-topped hills of the Lake Eyre basin and the mantle of gibbers that cover the far-reaching plains.

Chapter II

From Oodnadatta to Ernabella

WE LEFT OODNADATTA FOR the two hundred and eighty miles journey to the Musgrave Ranges at three o'clock (our schedule time was noon). 'Johnnie,' Lauri and I travelled in the front vehicle with the expedition gear; another lorry followed with the mails and supplies for the stations along the route.

The drivers, Alex and Charlie McLeod, told us that they hoped to reach Granite Downs, a hundred and fifty miles away, by three o'clock the following morning. At the time we thought it was a story for the city folk, but later learned that it might have been true, for the journey to the Musgraves and back had to be completed in about seventy hours, so that the return mails could catch the south-bound weekly train. As the trucks seldom reached the speed of twenty miles an hour, and often lumbered their way over the worst patches at three, there was obviously not much time for sleep. When wet weather or mechanical difficulties made the going even harder than usual, the drivers often travelled without rest.

The McLeod brothers were short men, not much above five feet six, and as lean as greyhounds. As drivers they were superb. They gathered speed whenever the track was suitable, but eased and coaxed their groaning lorries over the rough places, with a minimum of discomfort to the passengers and damage to their vehicles.

The first stage of our journey was across gibber plains, open flats and dry creek beds. Spotted round the flats were some picturesque stands of gidya trees (*Acacia cambagei*). My remark on their pleasing appearance brought forth a grudging assent from Charlie, a silence, and then—

'Gidya trees might be all right to look at, old man, though to smell them on a damp morning would spoil anyone's

8

breakfast; but gidya, after a camel has eaten it, and the beast has breathed on you—oh hell!'

Words failed him. I could almost feel his brain searching for a suitable term. He lit a cigarette and drove on in silence.

When we arrived at Todmorden Station it was almost dark. The manager's wife, brimming over with hospitality, sat us at a meal before a large fire and, while we ate, laughed, talked and exchanged the latest news and gossip of the Outback with us.

We left after about an hour and a half's stay, and as we bumped our way into the darkness my mind went back to our hostess at Todmorden, waiting perhaps for weeks for someone else to come along and break the monotony of the daily routine. The lot of the women in the bush is lonely to the extreme; yet the settlement of the empty spaces of Australia has largely been made possible by their self-sacrifice.

We drove on hour after hour, the whole world confined to the rough track brightly lit by the headlamps. On either side, blackness, inky blackness. The truck heaved, bumped and swayed from side to side. Charlie used his feet and hands continuously as he eased his vehicle over the rough boulders, across sandy creek beds, and steered between the gaunt desert trees that stood out brightly for a moment, then passed into oblivion. About ten o'clock our driver pointed into the darkness.

'Lambina Station used to be out there, but the big floods of 1939 got it. It had been raining for hours, and the blacks told the manager that he would have to shift to higher ground, but he wouldn't take any notice. The blacks always seem to know those things,' Charlie ruminated, as he changed gear and allowed his vehicle to run down the steep bank of a creek, 'and it's a pity he didn't take notice of the abos. It was darned rough on the woman and the youngsters.'

Then he told us, with frequent pauses, as he worked his way over the narrow gutters, cut by the flood, how first the water surrounded the house and started to trickle under the door, and how the family climbed up on the table. As the water rose higher, they were forced into the ceiling, and then on to the roof. Still the water rose, until the whole family, mother, father and three children, as well as three men from a nearby boring plant, had to shelter in the upper branches of a large gum tree. They stayed there for eighteen hours, drenched to the skin with the torrential rain, while their home and everything that belonged to them disappeared in the swirling, muddy waters. And when at last they escaped to higher ground, it was hours before either help or food could be obtained. The headlight beams still showed the debris of that flood, high in the branches of the gum trees.

Not many miles after we passed the deserted Lambina we reached the dreaded part of the journey, twenty miles of gibber and tableland country. Even the drivers were apprehensive of that section; we had heard them mention it several times on the way out. The track was frightful, crossed by short, steep gutters, and studded with rocks. The lorry would climb over some rough ridge, throwing us against each other in the tiny cabin, be eased down the other side; then with a clash of gears, groaning as if it were a living creature, the lorry would heave itself over the next obstacle. Every foot of the track had to be negotiated. Charlie's hands and feet were continually moving, steering, gear changing and braking the suffering vehicle.

By then I was travelling almost without thought. Except in the headlight, which revealed only obstacles to be crossed, there was nothing to be seen. My only relief was to watch the mounting miles on the dimly-lit speedometer; to see the decimals slowly turn to ten, the unit change, and the decimals start all over again. Another mile nearer the end of the nightmare track. It took us almost three hours to get through, and even Charlie, hard and tough as he was, kept me company in checking off the miles. He had been casting quick glances at my wife for some time, and, as soon as he ran out on the level plain, he stopped.

'It's well after midnight,' he said gruffly; 'can't make Granite Downs tonight, so get your camp gear off the lorry and have a sleep, but we must be going by four o'clock.'

No one needed a second telling. The sleeping-bags were quickly spread out, then a roaring fire lit, far too big for their bushman minds, but we were frozen to the bone. In a few minutes the billy was boiling, and the drivers and our own three selves were enjoying a cup of coffee and biscuits.

I slept the rest of a clear, frosty night—there was not much left—under a sky brilliant with twinkling stars. About four o'clock I built up the fire, and went across to the camp of the McLeods. To my surprise they were both asleep.

'What's up?' asked Charlie drowsily.

'We're ready to go on as soon as you are,' I said.

'For goodness sake get back to bed,' grumbled Charlie, 'and don't disturb the sleep of honest people.'

So back I went, for the bed was warm, the night cold, and I, like the drivers, had not had enough sleep. As we got to know the McLeods better, we found that they were true Aussies, and not to be taken too literally. Six o'clock, however, saw us packing up and moving off. The few hours of sleep had refreshed us remarkably, and life seemed good again.

From Granite Downs onward the track improved. The country was flatter, with more open valleys, covered thickly with silver, or mulga grass (*Anthistinia* sp.), which at that time of the year was dead and bleached a silvery white. That grass is an example of one of the many ways in which nature protects herself in the desert. The outer stalks, as they dry, bend inward, and twist over each other slightly, forming a kind of tent which shelters the still green base from the drying effects of the sun.

By the time we reached Moorilyanna, the distant outlines of the Musgrave Ranges, our destination, were showing blue and hazy on the horizon. At Moorilyanna we delivered a mail to an old bushman who had travelled in from the Everard Ranges, forty miles west. His vehicle was made from the chassis of a motor car, fitted with a pole so that it could be drawn by camels. Primitive, certainly, but simple, cheap and effective.

Waiting for us, sizzling away in the camp-oven, was a joint of mutton with some baked potatoes, and, beside the fire, as a dessert, a dish of ripe tomatoes (in June).

'Go and help yourselves,' our host called out hospitably, 'and don't be shy.'

While he unloaded his goods from the lorry we did as we were told, cut meat from the roasting joint, took our share of potatoes and enjoyed a good dinner.

After the harshness of the earlier stages of the journey, the beautiful park-like uplands, covered with silver grass and dotted with stands of the green pendulous-foliaged ironwood trees (*Acacia estrophiolata*), came as a welcome surprise. Indeed, the country was so like the fertile lands of Angaston or Eden Valley in South Australia that one expected each turn of the road to reveal a prosperous-looking farm house, with smoke curling from its chimneys, and the housewife feeding her fowls.

There were also many hundreds of young mulga trees (*Acacia aneura*) in all stages of growth, a sight which discounted the oft repeated story that the rabbits are destroying the seedlings of that desert acacia before they can become established. Charlie McLeod said, however, that mulga will not survive even a slight scorch from a bushfire, a fact which, no doubt, accounts for the numerous dead trees in the mulga scrubs.

It was half-past eight when we reached the Ernabella Mission Station, bitterly cold, and aching in every limb. We had been travelling for almost thirty hours over the roughest of roads, with scarcely six hours of sleep, and were pleased indeed to climb out of the lorry, knowing that one stage, at least, of our journey was over.

The whole Mission staff came out to welcome us, Mr. McDougall, who was in charge, Mr. and Mrs. Ward and Mr. and Mrs. Young, whose hospitality we were later to enjoy, and Mr. Trudinger, the teacher, who had already agreed to help in the research work.

"I had my first initiation into the gibber plains not far from Oodnadatta . . . ."
(Page 6.)

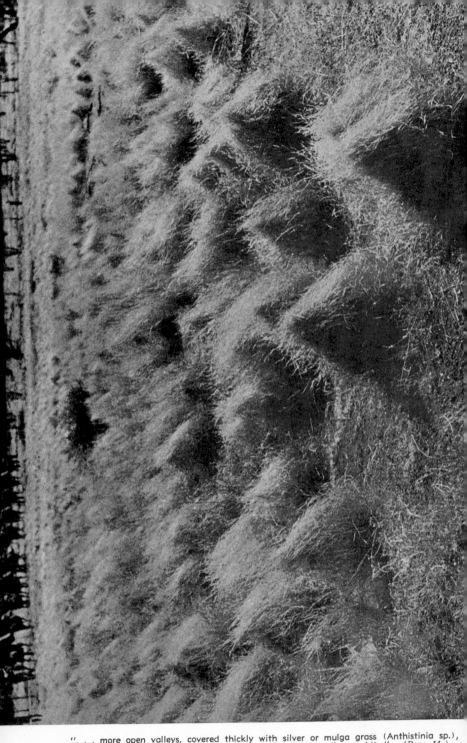

". . . more open valleys, covered thickly with silver or mulga grass (Anthistinia sp.),
which at that time of the year was dead and bleached to silvery white." (Page 11.)

When they left for their cosy firesides to read their long-awaited letters, we went to a nearby flat, unloaded our supplies and camping gear, and made ready for a meal. While the McLeods and ourselves stood round the fire, trying to get some warmth into our frozen bodies, and waiting for the billy to boil, we discussed the plans of the expedition, especially our means of transport.

'Got Tjundaga's camel string, eh?' said Alex. 'They're a poor lot, you know, so don't take any risks. They're either old crocks, or very young colts, and you can't push a string like that.'

'Be careful, too, about the waterholes in the Mann Ranges,' he added; 'they're tricky and unreliable. I've known some good bushmen to do a "perish" in that country.'

But the generosity of those men was revealed later.

'If you get into trouble out there,' said Alex, pointing westward in the darkness, 'send me word. Don't trouble about whether you can pay; just let me know, and I'll be out as soon as I possibly can.'

'Be careful, old man,' he added. 'You can't make many mistakes in that country and get back.'

We finished our meal, and said goodbye to the McLeod brothers, true bushmen to the core. Perhaps we may not see them again, but never shall we forget the generous offer they made to us city folk, whom they had known for less than two days.

I went to sleep under a clear sky, the Milky Way spanning the heavens, and a myriad stars twinkling, wondering what lay ahead of us in that strange land.

CHAPTER III

Our First Camp

WE WOKE TO SEE THE ROCKY
spinifex-covered hills of the Musgrave Ranges. The flat on
which we had camped was dotted with red granite outcrops,
intersected by creeks lined with green-foliaged eucalypts,
and carpeted with a thick growth of silver grass. On all
sides were pictures rich in form and colour. Everything, too,
was so quiet and peaceful, the quiet that makes one's mind
expand and grow, especially after the rush of weeks of
preparation, and the noise and strain of the long, tiring
journey.

Round us, on the other hand, was a scene of absolute
confusion. There were boxes of supplies, bags of flour,
scientific gear, and odds and ends everywhere, for it had
been pitch dark and freezing cold when we had unloaded,
and both we and the drivers were anxious to have a meal
and get to bed. To make things worse, we had dumped our
gear in a patch of bindy-eye (*Bassia longicuspis*)—a highly
improved form of the prickly-jack. We found those thorns
for days afterwards, in our bedclothes, in the bags, in the
boxes, and in all sorts of unexpected places. They were a
pest, and often did we curse them.

We chose a sandy patch at the junction of two creeks as
a camping place. It was a lovely spot, surrounded by large
white-barked gum trees (*Eucalyptus camaldulensis*). On one
side was a mass of jumbled boulders, a hundred feet high; on
the other, a level plain extending away to the foot of the
distant range.

As the mission folk were busy with their truck until the
evening, Lauri and I were faced with the arduous task of
carrying all the goods to our permanent camp, a distance
of about three hundred yards. The aboriginal men, how-

14

ever, came across to help us out of our difficulty, and soon
there was a line of naked helpers transporting our supplies.

The men carried almost everything on their heads, even
two hundred-pound bags of flour, for they seemed to have
little power in their hands; a four-gallon bucket of water
was an uncomfortable load. Their help left us free to put
up the tents, store the food, and nail boxes on the trees for
cupboards. By the late afternoon, when the Mission truck
arrived, the camp was shipshape and everything except a
few bags of flour safely stacked under shelter.

By that time the aboriginal women had completed their
daily food-gathering, and, with the men, were sitting in
groups watching the activities of the white folk. It soon,
became evident that something about my wife was puzzling
them beyond all else. Every time she moved out of her
tent, the women, giggling and excited, pointed to their heads,
while the men touched the back of their own, and then
waved their hands in her direction.

'It's certainly her hair,' said Lauri (it is long, and golden,
and was worn in a coil at the back of her neck), 'but it can't
be the colour that's attracting them. Mr. McDougall's hair
is much brighter than hers.'

Ron Trudinger, the teacher, solved the problem.

'No,' he said. 'It's not the colour that's puzzling them,
it's the style. She's using the head-dress of a man.'

Without knowing it, my wife had adopted a style of hair-
dressing that, in an aboriginal society, is used only by the
fully initiated men. They and they alone are allowed to
wear their hair, chignon fashion, on the back of their heads,
the women coiling theirs over the forehead. As the initiated
men are the important people, their privileges are strictly
guarded, and it was no small wonder that the infringement
of the rights by a woman, even though unwittingly committed, should have caused so much comment.

'What about taking down your hair?' asked the teacher.
'The natives want to see how long it is.'

'Johnnie,' after some little hesitation, did so. With a
torrent of chatter, and cries of wonder, some sixty people

left their nearby camp, crossed the sandy creek-bed in a body, and surrounded my wife; mothers with babies across their hips, men with spears and spear-throwers in their hands, and children everywhere. I knew little of their language at that time, but sufficient to hear the women speaking excitedly of 'long hair' and 'like the sunlight.' One old man was particularly puzzled. He walked round and round 'Johnnie,' looking at her with a comical, puzzled expression, as though trying to decide whether or not her hair was real. He even put out his hand to touch it, but withdrew quickly, either not daring, or not wishing to be so familiar.

'Johnnie' was overwhelmed by so much attention. She had not expected anything like that to happen; and it took the combined pleading of both Lauri and myself to keep her 'on stage' for more than a minute or two. Finally, unable to bear the strain of so many peering eyes, she fled to her tent, and the show was over.

The day following, Tjundaga, our half-caste guide and interpreter, came in with his string of camels. Alex McLeod was right when he described them as poor. They most certainly were. There was only one decent-looking beast in the string, and two, in particular, were so thin that it was a puzzle how they kept alive. I wondered how such a string would stand up to the long and difficult journeys ahead of us.

Tjundaga was a member of the Aranda tribe, but could speak the language of the Pitjendadjara tribe, the people among whom we were going to work.

Nibiana, his wife, was a young, happy-faced aboriginal woman, who, although she had been brought up and trained as a cook by the wife of a station owner, was far happier roaming from place to place with her husband. She appointed herself our kitchen assistant, and improved the camp by building a wind-break and a bush-shelter under which we could have our meals.

As many of the aborigines of the Pitjendadjara tribe, whose life, art and customs we had set out to investigate, were camping nearby, we planned to stay at Ernabella for

We woke to see the rocky, spinifex-covered hills of the Musgrave Ranges." *(Page 14.)*

" . . . Kinari to look after the camels."   *(Page 18.)*

a month to gather the ethnological data that would deter-
mine our future movements.

On a previous expedition I had found the most effective
means of gaining that information was to give the men sheets
of brown paper and coloured crayons, and ask them to draw.
With those materials they would illustrate, by primitive
sketches, their tribal country and the legends associated with
it. That data would enable us to decide the route of the
expedition and the native informants we would take with us.

Work then started in earnest. Each morning Tjundaga
and I went across to the school, with sheets of brown paper
in our hands and crayons in our pockets, for Ron Trudinger
had generously allotted me an hour each day to collect
drawings from the children. During the month we were at
Ernabella the aboriginal children, from four to fourteen
years of age, made almost three hundred sheets of drawings
for us. Simple they undoubtedly were, and, to my great
satisfaction, showed no signs of European influence, for the
school had only been established a few months. This col-
lection is unique, for the school life and the illustrated
papers would soon have shown the children new ways of
depicting their mental images.

I used to enjoy my morning visit to the school house, and
the sight of so many happy faces, some of whom I was to
know well as time went on. The children were taught to
read and write in their own language, but to calculate in
our numerals, theirs being limited to four.

I don't think that they enjoyed the reading and writing
any more than I used to do. It was most unlikely that the
youngsters could place any value on that training, when, so
far as they knew, the whole of their future would be given
over to hunting, food-gathering and their ceremonial life.
Although I doubted the wisdom of teaching the aboriginal
children to read and write in a language that had no literature, I could not but be impressed with the affection that
Ron Trudinger bore towards his little pupils, and the manner
in which it was reciprocated. Whenever we saw the teacher

c

he was surrounded by a crowd of children, hanging on to his coat, his hands and his wrists.

One holiday, Ron Trudinger arranged to take us with him on a school picnic. There was much chatter and excitement round our camp that morning, for a respite from school is always a gala day for children, be they brown or white, especially as, on that occasion, many of the little folk were going for their first camel ride.

We had planned to start early, but that was not to be. Some of the kiddies had forgotten their issue of flour—no small wonder, when they knew just where to gather an abundance of native food; others had been sent to get the horse, which, judging from his antics, had a distinct objection to picnics; and the camels, if their moans and cries were an indication of their feelings, had similar ideas. So, what with rounding up the beasts, hanging packages on the camels, and assembling the children, it was well into the middle of the morning before we moved off.

It was a procession not often seen by city folk. Besides the children, there were three supercilious camels, totally disdainful of their human freight; a small black pony, somewhat nervous of its little riders; four white people, and two aboriginal men, Kinari and Jabiaba, to look after the camels.

The camels were fully laden. On the leader was 'Johnnie,' with one child before and another behind her, and everywhere they could be tied were slabs of raw meat, billycans and small bags of flour. Lauri's camel was groaning under a similar load, and the third was lined with kiddies, six of them. Those who could hung on to some part of the saddle; those who could not clung to their companions like limpets. How they stayed there was a puzzle, but they did, and enjoyed the experience immensely. The children who walked were not distressed, for they knew their turn to have a ride would come later. Some jogged along beside the teacher and me, holding our hands, and chattering happily in their native tongue; others roamed the open plain collecting honey-bearing flowers, tubers, or small desert creatures.

Lauri had an embarrassing moment when one little chap handed him some squirming white wood-grubs, a repulsive looking present for one not yet initiated into the appreciation of aboriginal dainties.

It was midday before we reached the steep-sided Intjinbidi gorge, where a watercourse had cut its way through the main range. Kinari and Jabiaba stayed behind with the camels, and the rest of the party scrambled up the rocky ledges to eat their lunch near an upper spring.

Neidi, a boy about twelve, appointed himself my wife's escort. He helped her over the rough, tumbled boulders, offered her his hand in the steepest places, and pointed out the best footholds, watching carefully lest she should slip. It was an incongruous yet pleasing sight; the lithe, naked aboriginal boy attending my wife with all the courtesy that one would accord a queen. The incident, unusual as it seemed to us at the time, was but one of the many examples of courtesy we later experienced while living with those native people.

Near a small rock-hole on one of the upper levels of the gorge the children lit a fire and cooked their dampers from the flour that was almost left behind, and grilled the meat that had decorated 'Johnnie's' camel on the outward journey. The children took little care to see that the food was well cooked; the damper was largely dough, and the meat little more than scorched. But what matter, their teeth and digestion were more than equal to the task.

When the meal was finished the children started to play, for, after all, why else should one go to a picnic? The boys began the spear and disc game. Already some of them had made a number of short spears from a tecoma vine which was growing on the rocky walls of the gorge, while others had cut a disc of thick green bark, about the size of a dinner plate, from a nearby gum tree. The players then formed themselves into two groups, and took up positions about fifteen yards apart on the floor of the gorge. As the disc was rolled backward and forward between them, each group in turn tried to spear the target as it passed. There did not seem to be any spirit of competition, either between the boys themselves, or the groups; their enjoyment was gained from the success in spearing the bark disc.

The game provided not only enjoyment but training for the boys, for by it they acquired that quickness of eye and accuracy of aim that would be so essential to them in later life, when they, the boys of today, would be the hunters and food-gatherers of tomorrow, and the target, not the rolling disc, but the quickly moving animals of the desert.

It was while photographing from a jutting rock, some thirty feet above the players, that I noticed the picturesqueness of the scene below. The boys had chosen a level pavement on the floor of the gorge as their pitch. A shaft of light from the late afternoon sun, coming through a gap in the hills, illuminated that pavement with all the brilliance of a powerful spot-light, leaving everything else in deep shadow. In the middle of the scene, like actors on a stage, were twenty or more naked brown-skinned children, their bodies almost luminous in that brilliant light; some poised like bronze statues as they waited, tense and eager to spear the oncoming disc; others were running, jumping and laughing from sheer joy, and the excitement of the game.

We made a late start for home, and by sunset were still a long way from camp. The children were tired, for, like all of their kind, they had not stopped the whole day long. To add to their discomfort an icy cold wind had started to blow when darkness set in. We white folk walked to keep ourselves warm, leaving the horse and the camels free to carry the children. The beasts were again full laden, two or more children on the horse and five on each of the camels, where all, except those on the ends of the line, were kept warm by the contact of the bodies of their companions. 'Johnnie' had a child about ten years old tucked under her cloak, and Lauri and I had two each under our overcoats, one on either side, their arms round our waists, ours round their shoulders. I was surprised how easy it was to walk with those little chaps; they timed the rhythm of my step perfectly.

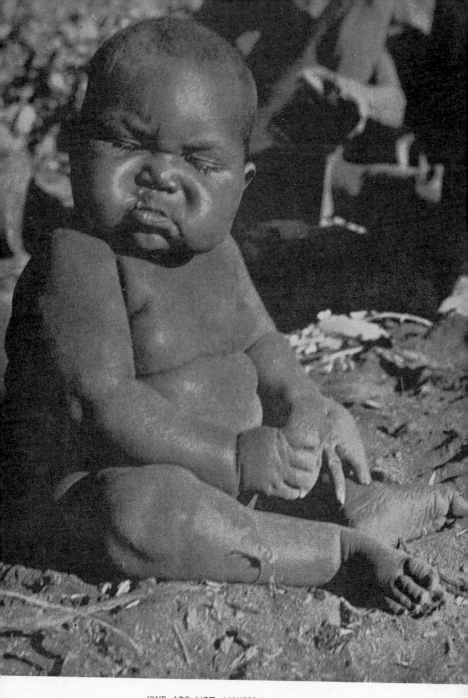

"WE ARE NOT AMUSED"

"We grew very fond of those children . . . and left them with more than a passing regret." *(Page 21.)*

CEREMONY OF THE MOUNTAIN DEVIL
(a) Banded Sleepy-Lizard (Tiliqua scincoides).   (b) Mountain Devil (Moloch horridus).   *(Page 24.)*

It was pitch dark when we reached our camp, and while we enjoyed the meal of euro tail stew, so thoughtfully prepared by Nibiana, we could hear the excited chattering of the children, telling their parents about the events of the day.

The wealth of affection that exists between the adults and the children in an aboriginal tribe has to be seen to be believed. There was one baby boy in camp, perhaps nine months old, who was seldom in his mother's arms except for meals. At all other times some man, woman, boy or girl was either carrying him about or playing with him. The older children seemed to go their own sweet way, without hindrance from anyone.

The little folk sat round our fire at all times of the day, yet, in spite of the apparent lack of discipline by the parents, they were not the slightest trouble, any request that we made being obeyed with perfect good humour. There were sweets, sugar and all sorts of dainties in open cupboards, only a few feet from where they used to sit, yet no child touched them.

We grew very fond of those children, and when the time came, we left them with more than a passing regret.

CHAPTER IV

The Mountain-devil Ceremony

NOT LONG AFTER OUR ARRIVAL
the old men established a camp close to our own, and, at my
request, started to make drawings on sheets of brown paper.

Although the sketches collected at the school by Tjundaga
and myself gave us a unique record of the developing
symbolism of primitive children, those of the old men were
a veritable storehouse of knowledge, for they illustrated the
legends of the tribe, the exploits of their mythical forebears,
and the secret aspects of their life. Another point of interest
was the unusually archaic symbols employed in the drawings,
symbols which bore more than a passing resemblance to the
designs of the early cave paintings of Europe.

The fact that Tjundaga had passed through all stages of
his initiation was a great help in our research, for, as I had
found on previous expeditions, once the aborigines accepted
me as trustworthy, they talked freely about their tribal
secrets, provided those facts were known to the interpreter.
Had Tjundaga not been fully initiated, the men would
have feigned ignorance of everything dealing with their
ceremonies beyond his knowledge.

Every day Tjundaga and I attended the fireside of our
aboriginal informants, collected the sheets of drawings they
produced, drawings that illustrated, almost without exception, the legends of the creation of their country.

The creation stories of the world provide a fascinating
study for ethnologists. Those current in the western civilizations, which originated among the early Semites of the
lower Euphrates, bear little resemblance to the aborigines'
conception of their beginnings. Their Genesis has no story
of an ideal existence, and man's fall from a state of per-
fection, but is composed of a number of legendary tales

22

which describe how the world was made by their mighty progenitors.

In the beginning, or the 'Dreaming Times' as old Nanta-wana poetically described the creation period, there was no life upon the world; no creatures, no trees, no plants, not even a mountain, low hill or watercourse. The world was a huge plain extending level and featureless on all sides as far as the eye could see. At some time, so long ago that old Nantawana could not find a simile, the *tjukurita* men came, giant, semi-human creatures, who seem to have thought and acted like human beings, but resembled, in appearance, various animals, birds, plants or insects. These *tjukurita* or ancestral men travelled extensively over the countryside, and, wherever they performed their everyday tasks, making fire, camping, digging for water, such as are carried out by the aborigines today, some natural feature rose out of the bare flat land.

Everything in the world, except the level earth, is the result of the activities and wanderings of those giant beings. The waterhole at Ayers Rock, where later we filled our canteens, was the place where huge snakes had camped; the gorge at Nirunya, Jabiaba's country, had been torn out in mythical times by Milbili, the Lizard, in his pursuit of the woman Kutunga; and the immense domes at Katatjuta (Mt. Olga) were once the camps of the man-eating Pungalunga men. Those great creators of the lands of the aborigines were, at the same time, the forebears of the tribe. So that, in the aboriginal tribes of today there are Snake-men, Emu-men, Ant-men, and so on, all of whom believe they are directly descended from one or another of the *tjukurita* men of the long distant past. Tjundaga, my interpreter, was a Perentie- (large lizard) man from Undiara; Jabiaba, a Kangaroo-man from Puka; and Moanya, a Wonambi- (mythical snake) man from Piltadi.

Since everyone in the tribe claims descent from one or the other of those mythical beings, the *tjukurita* men, and each in turn lives in the land created by them, it naturally follows that each man, woman and child is closely linked both by lineage and legend with his surroundings, the ranges, the rocks, the trees and the watercourses. They are his, the work of his ancestors, and proud he is to show them to the appreciative visitor.

Only those who know the close link between the native people and their land can realize the heartache and sorrow they suffer when driven from their homes, and the homes of generations before them, because the land is wanted by the white man for his sheep and cattle. As the aborigines so love their native land, and so cherish the legends of their origin, it is natural that the drawings of the aboriginal men should deal with their creation stories. Interpreting these primitive sketches was a lengthy business, but they gave us a wealth of knowledge and an insight into their life.

Then one day Jabiaba made a drawing that explained why many of the small lizards and birds have their present-day markings. At the time of creation, the Mountain-devil[1] (a fearsome looking, beautifully coloured, but perfectly harmless lizard) invited the smaller birds and reptiles to a ceremony at Miniri (the place of the Mountain-devil), a low hill in the desert country south of the Mann Ranges.

The little creatures came from near and far, for it was even worse manners than it is now to refuse such an invitation. And so they came, the Bell-bird, the Spinifex-wren, the Willy-wagtail, the Bower-bird, the Ringneck-parrot, and a host of larger and smaller reptiles. After the introductions were made the Mountain-devil, who was the leader of the ceremony, instructed the visitors to pair off and decorate each other for the coming rituals. The Spinifex-wren painted the Willy-wagtail, the Bell-bird the Blue-wren, the Stumped-tailed Lizard one of his own kind, and likewise all the other little creatures. The Banded Sleepy-Lizard[2] and the Mountain-devil took special care over their decorations, for each had an important part to play.

Because of the late arrival of many of the ancestral people, and the fact that introductions had taken longer than was expected, the sun had set before their tasks were finished.

1 *Moloch horridus.*   2 *Tiliqua scincoides.*

The Blue-wren had already been decorated by the Bell-bird and was so pleased with the result that he was anxious to make his friend as colourful as himself. It was, however, too dark for him to see properly, so he lit a clump of spinifex nearby to provide sufficient light. Unfortunately, at the same time, a strong wind sprang up and caused the fire to spread rapidly over the countryside. It destroyed the trees, it blackened the hills, and practically surrounded the little creatures at Miniri. Many of them just escaped with their lives.

That disastrous fire spoiled the glossy-white plumage of all the birds. Most of the feathers of the Willy-wagtail were burnt black, and those of the Mud-lark were scorched in many places. The heat turned the Spinifex-wren a rusty red, and the smoke so dyed the breast of the Blue-wren that it retains its colour even to the present day. The eyes of the Stumped-tailed Lizard smarted so badly that the tears ran down from the corners in streams. Any aborigine will show you the marks if you ask him.

The Banded Sleepy-lizard and the Mountain-devil escaped unhurt, and still wear their ceremonial colours. The Mountain-devil, however, fared even better, for he not only retained his markings, but also his ceremonial dress of decorated sticks. Even now you can see them on his body as long spikes. And, should you hold him upright, the little chap will put his hands in front of his face, as if to shield it from the heat of the fire so carelessly lit by the Blue-wren.

That legend formed the basis for the first ceremony belonging to the boys. It was essentially their own. The older men did not take part, and the women were not allowed to go near. Newly initiated youths, themselves little more than boys, taught the lads the dances, the chants, and the designs which custom had decreed must be painted on their bodies.

I do not know whether it was our special interest in the legends, or whether the time was ripe for the rituals, but, the evening following the day that Jabiaba made the drawing, Pilala, a young man, with a great show of secrecy, whispered to me:

'*Tjitji inma* (boys' ceremony) tomorrow morning, early fella.'

That was good news, for, as yet, we had no knowledge of the ceremonial life of the younger boys; in fact, up till then we did not know that there was one. I went to bed that evening filled with anticipation of what we might see next morning.

Before sunrise we heard the sound of chanting behind a pile of rocks some distance away. There we found a number of boys painting each other, under the supervision of two young men, Niari and Pilala. Pilala was himself in charge of the rituals, and represented the Mountain-devil, while the other boys, ranging from seven to thirteen years, were already being decorated by their companions. As in the legend, the boys stood in pairs, the Spinifex-wren and the Willy-wagtail, the Bell-bird and the Blue-wren, and large and small Stumped-tailed Lizards, and many others. One of the older boys, who impersonated the Banded Sleepy-lizard, painted the leader, the Mountain-devil, who, like the people in the myth, returned the compliment.

Each boy had been greased, then rubbed over with powdered red ochre from top to toe. On that base was drawn the symbolic design which indicated the bird or reptile that the boy represented. The brushes used were no more than a finger, or a piece of bark stripped from a nearby tree, and the pigments, red ochre, charcoal and white pipe-clay, ground to a powder on a flat stone and mixed with water.

When those preparations were completed, the boys lined up behind a corkwood tree ready for the dance, which portrayed how the visiting creatures approached the camp of the Mountain-devil in mythical times. To the chanting of Pilala and Niari, the boys danced with prancing footsteps toward the singers, their bodies bent forward at the hips, and each hand passing over the other, with a curious rotating motion. Every now and again they stopped, called out in a highly excited tone—as did the ancestral creatures when they approached the camp of their host—then continued until, with a grand flourish, they concluded their performance in the front of the leaders. The leaders and the boys then formed themselves into a tight, compact group, and paraded, first to the aboriginal women, then to my wife, who returned the compliment paid to her by a gift of dried fruit and sweets.

Pilala told us later that the performance would be continued next morning, so, before retiring, we laid everything out in readiness for an early start. We were anxious not to miss the preliminary phases of the body decorations, as we had done on the first morning.

At early dawn I was awakened by a low, moaning sound that seemed to come from the whole camp. I dressed quickly, called Lauri, grabbed note-book and cameras, and rushed across to where Jabiaba was sleeping.

'Wha' for you bin wake me?' grumbled the old man.

'I bin think that one noise belonga boys' ceremony,' I said.

'You big fool, Tjamu' (my native name), complained Jabiaba. 'That noise no more *tjitji inma*' (boys' ceremony); 'that one made by blackfella. Him cry because him sorry longa Katanya's husband.'

We went back to our camp feeling somewhat abashed, for not only had Jabiaba, but several of the other men, made it quite clear that neither our visit nor our continued presence was desired. In our hurry we had not realized that the sound we had heard was the mass expression of grief over the death of Namana, Katanya's husband. As we prepared our breakfast in the cold light of dawn the sounds of grief died down, and quiet again stole over the camp.

About sunrise, Jabiaba, true to his promise, sent a little chap across to tell us that the *tjitji inma* was about to start. On that morning the ceremonies were unlike those of the previous day. The boys were painted, but with different symbols, and the dances were individual impersonations of the ancestral beings associated with the birds and lizards. In one of those, Niari danced and acted the part of a Bat ancestor, who was trying to hide from a Lizard-man travelling to the Mountain-devil's ceremony.

Niari was almost blind, the result of some destructive eye disease introduced by our white civilization. His sight was too dim for him to be a successful hunter, the ambition of all aboriginal youths, nor could he even see to find food on the ground. He was pathetically anxious to help 'Johnnie' with the camp chores, and to make drawings for me, although, poor man, he could barely see the lines he drew. He was one of those sad discards that one finds in any civilization, shy, diffident, and acutely aware of his failings. But in his acting he was superb. In that field he could express himself to the full, with all the joy and confidence that came from the knowledge that he was the equal, if not the superior, of his companions.

His dancing was beautiful to see, and, to me, was comparable with that of some of the performers in the great ballets which have visited Australia. True, the backdrop was but a pile of red granite boulders, illuminated by the early light of morning, the stage a grass-covered flat, and the actor, a naked, brown man, his greased body shining in the yellow sunlight.

He danced the story of the little Bat-man, who had attempted to escape the Lizard people. The furtive movements of Niari, as he crept stealthily from tree to tree, his low crouching in the grass, or graceful bounds over the scattered rocks, had all the fervour, the abandon, and the unselfconsciousness of the true artist. For those few minutes he belonged to the dim, ghostly past; he was one of the strange inhabitants of long ago, not the half-blind, despised Niari of the present.

After that dramatic performance, pairs of younger boys impersonated, first, two ancestral women travelling, then a pair of Marsupial-men catching butterflies as they passed along. The youngsters danced in time to the music, with high prancing steps, pausing now and again to mime the actions of their ancestral forebears.

CEREMONY OF THE MOUNTAIN DEVIL

". . . the other boys, ranging from seven to thirteen years, were already being decorated by their companions." *(Page 26.)*

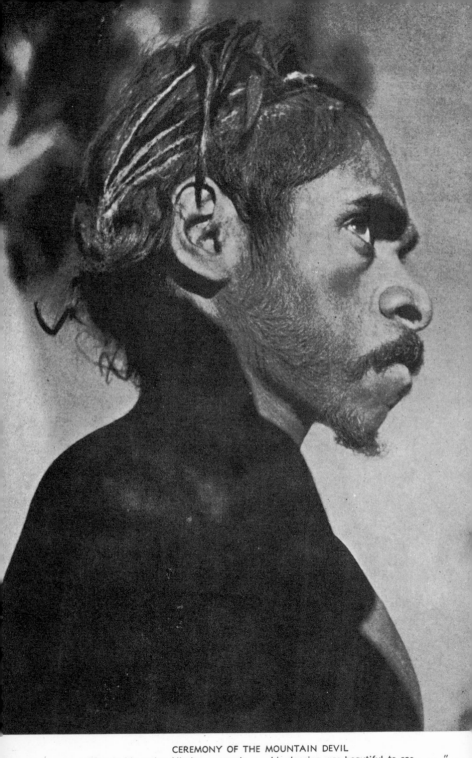

CEREMONY OF THE MOUNTAIN DEVIL
"But in his acting Niari was superb . . . his dancing was beautiful to see . . . ."
(Page 28.)

Then, while the chanting broke out afresh, the boys, some only seven years old, ran forward and danced a curious, shuffling step in front of the singers. It was obvious that the youngest of them had not previously taken part in those rituals, for he was particularly awkward with his feet, and extremely self-conscious. Pilala made him practise the step several times before he was allowed to go.

Again, as on the previous morning, the boys ran to the women's camp to show themselves, then to 'Johnnie' for approval—and sweets—and, without waiting for another minute, off to school, for it was a Monday.

From a school of their culture to one of ours. What a change! In theirs, the open air, the joy of song and bodily movement, backed by a greater wealth of drama and mythology than we can ever realize; in ours, sitting still out of the sunlight, slaving at symbols and figures that are entirely unrelated to their daily needs.

That evening we saw the finale of the proceedings. My wife was invited specially by the women, for, on that occasion all took a part. The performance had started by the time we arrived. The lads, seated round a central fire, were chanting the songs to which the men and women danced. It was a pleasing sight, the keen, alert faces of the boys, dimly visible in the fitful light of the fire, oblivious to everything but the chanting of their ancient songs and the acting of their sides.

The women took but little part in that evening's programme, or, for that matter, at any time. They did not sit in the circle round the fire, but in scattered groups on the outskirts. Again they had but one dance, in which they shuffled their feet, with their hips held rigidly, and thrust forward, and arms swinging freely, their feet making parallel ridges in the sand as they moved along. Simple that dance undoubtedly was, but it was their own, and they gained much enjoyment from it.

The men, on the other hand, in all but the boys' ceremonies, not only led the singing, but did the acting, portraying with amazing skill the whole range of human emotions, from the sheer mimicry of daily events to the highly formalized and exacting dances of the sacred ceremonials. That evening, I should say, they danced humorous incidents of the past, for each act brought forth roars of laughter from the assembled people.

I knew, in only a fragmentary way, the significance behind that miming, and I did not enquire. For that night at least I gave myself over to the joy of seeing something both strange and beautiful. I again felt the sheer loveliness of movement and form as when I had seen Pavlova, Algeranoff, and, that morning, Niari. It was all there. The singers, beating the ground to mark the rhythm of the dance, all keyed up and excited; the actors, magnificent specimens of manhood, posturing and dancing in the flickering firelight; and both singers and dancers conscious of nothing but their art and their ancient stories.

It was late when we left, but still the dancing went on, the lads beating the time, while the men danced, and danced again, with unabated enthusiasm.

CHAPTER V

The Ceremonial Life

THE CEREMONY OF THE
Mountain-devil, and the stories belonging to it, give the
boys a foretaste of the rich world of song and drama that
awaits them. Throughout the whole of their childhood, both
the boys and the girls are surrounded by all the love and
affection that one could wish for them. They wander in
little groups, playing in the creek beds, hunting for titbits of
food, or resting beside their tiny fires, singing their childish
songs. Their parents do not punish and seldom chide them,
nor do they restrict the wanderings of the little people,
unless they approach the old men when they are discussing
ceremonial matters. Altogether, except for the hardships
that Nature inflicts on them during the long desert journeys,
it would be difficult to imagine a more ideal social condition
for any child.

Although the older boys know, in a vague way, that many
trials and painful ordeals await them, they are not unduly
troubled, but, like all children, enjoy the present to the full,
letting the future look after itself.

One evening, however, the happy, care-free life of one
of their number is completely shattered. Closely related
women, his source of comfort in every childish trouble, suddenly attack him, and, with blazing firesticks, drive him from
the camp. By that ceremonial expulsion the lad is deprived
of the affection and indulgence of the women, and forced to
live under the dominance of the gruff, unresponsive old men,
his tutors on the long, difficult road to tribal manhood. From
then, until the circumcision ceremonies are completed, perhaps in a year or so, the youth is treated as an outcast. He
always sleeps at some distance from the main camp; never
goes near or calls out to the women; nor does he speak to
the old men, unless first addressed, and then his reply must
not be above a whisper. It is a most drastic break, and the

31

youth must be thoroughly puzzled and distressed over the many prohibitions that have so quickly surrounded him.

But, drastic as this change undoubtedly is, the aboriginal system of education shows considerable wisdom. The boys are allowed to develop freely in an almost ideal environment until the bodily changes and mental turmoil of adolescence are stabilized. It is then, and then only, that they commence their long, rigorous training for manhood.

For perhaps a year, the ostracised youth travels with the men during the day, and sleeps beside his tiny fires on the outskirts of the camp at night. He lives from day to day, knowing that, at some uncertain time, he will undergo that mysterious experience which will change him from a boy to a man. The vague and highly coloured stories circulating among his youthful companions make him fear the ordeals of initiation. Nevertheless, he looks forward to them, knowing that without those trials he cannot attain tribal manhood, the goal of every aboriginal youth.

Eventually the day comes when he is pounced upon by the old men, and, to the accompaniment of the wailing of the women and the shouting and stamping of the already initiated men, he is led to the secret grounds.

During the initiation rituals, the men who stand in close relationship to him open the veins in their arms and allow the blood to pour over his body. The fundamental idea behind this custom is that blood is *kuranita* (life essence), and the giving of ample supplies of blood will provide the initiate with the necessary health and vitality to grow to strong and virile manhood.

Initiation, in an aboriginal society, marks the transition from care-free youth to disciplined manhood; from irresponsibility to obligation; and from ignorance to enlightenment. Its rituals are designed to teach the youth, by primitive symbolism and strange ceremonies, the rules and philosophies of the tribe, and the prohibitions that accompany them. Nothing is neglected that will help to bring about those results; ordeals of pain, trials of fortitude, the air of mystery and concealment, all emphasizing the importance

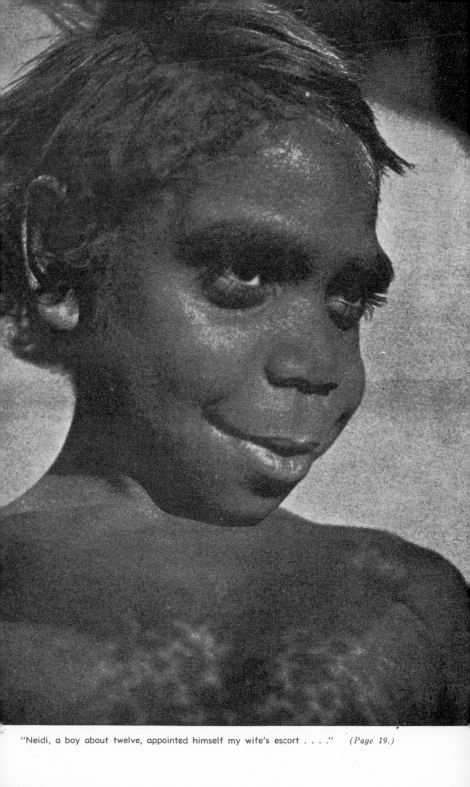

"Neidi, a boy about twelve, appointed himself my wife's escort . . . ."   (Page 19.)

"When the meal was finished the children started to play."   (Page 19.)

of that crisis. The youth, lying face downward, hears, but does not see the rituals enacted at his side, except when the guardian, by the aid of the flickering firelight, allows him a glimpse of some awe-inspiring spectacle. So deeply impressed is the receptive mind of the initiate by those strange experiences, that neither they, nor their associated meanings, can ever be forgotten.

The first initiation ceremony, which includes the rite of circumcision, is the youth's most important step toward manhood. At its completion he wears a distinctive head-dress, is given a special name that marks his social progress, and travels only with the old men, who act as both tutors and guardians. He must neither see nor be seen by the women; indeed he is, as his new name 'Wangarapa' indicates, 'a boy in hiding.' With the old men, he now makes long journeys to attend the ceremonies of other people, although he himself may be forbidden to see any but the least sacred of them. But in spite of that, his continual wanderings, and the instructions of the old men, make him conversant not only with the tribal myths, but also with the topography associated with them.

The zeal with which the initiate enters into that new world of song and ceremony, and the learning of the stories and rules of the tribe, is remarkable. He practises continuously with his fellow initiates not only the songs, but the dances that accompany them. Through these a new world is revealed. He then understands the history of his tribal lands, of which formerly he had no knowledge, and the actions of his elders previously incomprehensible to his uninstructed mind. By the time these wanderings are finished the lad is fully grown, and ready to pass through the final stages of initiation, the sub-incision rite.

This rite is the badge of a fully tribalized man. At its completion he is allowed to marry, if his promised wife is old enough; he may sit in the tribal council, although he will have little power; and he can actively participate in some, but not all, of the rituals. It will be many years before the newly created member can learn all the tribal secrets.

D

Even Moanya, who was already showing grey hairs, could not answer some of my questions.

'I am not old enough,' he said; 'ask Jabiaba.'

Although the sub-incision rite is the most painful of the ordeals, and the one that actually admits the initiate to full manhood status, there is little or no mythology or ceremony associated with it. From this fact it would seem that the curious and unexplainable custom has only recently become part of the tribal pattern, and has not yet had time to develop its own mythology. Indeed most, if not all, of the songs and dances used in connection with it are borrowed from the rich field of the circumcision ceremonies.

The aboriginal ceremonies (known to most people as corroborees), of which the initiation rituals are but a part, are the dramatic representations of the legendary stories of the tribe in music and mime. They have several functions: they instruct the people in the beliefs of the tribe, particularly the youths through their initiation; they control the complicated forces of nature by strange magical rites, and so provide adequate food and water; and they enact the simpler myths that explain the creation of the plants, the animals, the sky and the land. Whereas most of the songs which dramatize the legendary stories are the personal property of the aborigines owning the land to which the songs relate, those of the initiation rituals are both known and sung by all the full members of the tribe.

But those initiatory songs, regarded as being particularly sacred, are never mentioned in the presence of the youths or the women, nor sung within their hearing. They deal with the adventures of three ancestral heroes—Malu, the kangaroo; Kunjula, the euro (a hill kangaroo); and Tjulki, a little night owl.

These three are the most important ancestral beings in the aboriginal pantheon, for not only did they create many creeks, waterholes and ranges, but they also laid down the laws and ceremonies that govern the two main issues of the aborigines' existence, initiation and burial, the entrance into manhood and the departure therefrom.

The wanderings and exploits of these ancestors are commemorated in a long series of chants and dramatic dances that form the groundwork on which the circumcision rituals are based. Both the words and the music of these chants are exceptionally simple, the text seldom exceeding eight words —although there are innumerable verses—and the music a limited melody that starts on a high note and follows a gradually descending scale until it ends, almost in a growl. Although many of these songs may seem monotonous to the unaccustomed ear of the white man, the 'big' songs, as the aborigines call them, chanted at important stages in the progress of initiation are spirited and stimulating.

One of the duties of the native in charge of the circumcision rites is, not only to lead the chanting of the songs, but to be sure they are sung in the correct order, for it is an almost unforgivable offence to chant a 'line of songs' in the wrong sequence. Some men practise their songs days beforehand, so that when they reach the ceremonial ground they will be 'word perfect.'

In the initiation ceremonies, in fact throughout the whole of the tribal organization, the people are divided into two classes, the *tamaniltjan* and the *nanunduraka*. That grouping governs all aspects of their life, marriage, social relationships and patterns of behaviour. I had been admitted as a member of the tribe, therefore one half of the people were *tamaniltjan* to me, or to use a well-worn but expressive outback term, they were 'my mob.' The other class, the *nanunduraka*, were the 'outsiders.' Marriage within the group is forbidden; that is, one's wife must be an 'outsider'. Marriage within the group is unthinkable; it would be equivalent to living with one's own sister.

Although the dual division of the tribe is not evident to the casual observer, it stands out in sharp relief in the initiation ground. Both the men who perform the initiatory operation and the group in charge of the proceedings are of the opposite class to the initiate, and even in the chanting of the songs the two divisions sit in different circles.

I have seen the initiation rituals in all their stages; it was a great honour to be thus trusted. But as the aborigines believe that dire misfortune will befall the tribe if the secrets of the initiation ground become known to women, the details of the secret life of the men will be reserved for scientific journals.

When, however, I saw the dramatization of the myth of the Wild Turkey, the ancestral being who tried to steal fire from mankind, I was under no such obligation.

The acting was very different from that in the secret rituals. Many phases of initiation have become formalized and stable, because of their continual repetition and ancient usage, but the drama of the Wild Turkey seemed to be less fettered by such traditions. There were no extensive preparations, few body markings and no blood letting. Nor were there any stage aids of any kind; no darkness with flickering firelight to help the illusion; no grotesque figures to stimulate the imagination; not even a clump of trees from which the actors might appear; just an open grass-covered plain, and a few low mulga trees. Yet, I shall never forget that afternoon, so vivid an impression did the performance create. I have often wondered since why I was so impressed. I left the ceremonial ground with the glowing sensation of having seen something beautiful, as I have felt after a performance by some artist of our culture.

A crayon drawing made by old Tjalerina was responsible for the experience. It revealed the legend explaining how in 'Creation Times' a mythical Wild Turkey-man had tried to steal fire from mankind.

However, long, long ago, as they say in the European fairy tales, the aborigines of the Petermann Ranges owned a desert oak that burned continuously, yet was never consumed. It was the only fire in the world and much valued by its aboriginal owners. For, should their camp fire go out through storm or carelessness, they could visit the burning log and kindle their fires afresh.

In those days there lived a particularly unpleasant old Wild Turkey-man, Kipara, who, because he had a minor

INITIATION CEREMONY

"Initiation in an aboriginal society marks the transition from care-free youth to disciplined manhood." *(Page 32.)*

INITIATION CEREMONY

(a) "The youth, lying face-downward, hears but does not see the rituals enacted at his side . . . ." (Page 33.)

(b) ". . . rituals are designed to teach the youth . . . the rules and philosophies of the tribe." (Page 32.)

quarrel with the owners of the fire, planned to steal and dip it in the sea. Had he been successful, a dire calamity would have overtaken the world. No longer could the aborigines have warmed themselves during the cold winter nights, or lighted their way in the darkness. A cold, dreary world would have faced the human race had it not been for the initiative of two Hawk-men, who, at the last moment, snatched the firestick from the vengeful old scoundrel.

The legend of the fire stealing, widespread in aboriginal mythology, always finishes with the downfall of the culprit and the restoration of the fire. Some of the coastal tribes believe that it was the Fire-tailed Finch which saved the fire, and that the red spot on its rump is the result of the burn received by the courageous little bird as it carried the glowing stick from the thief to its original owners.

The dramatization of the legend was divided into eight acts, each of which had a single chant as a basis. Four dealt with the legend of the Wild Turkey and the firestick, and the other four, supposedly composed by Kipara himself, described some of the experiences on his long journey. A circle of men chanted the songs, beating the ground with sticks to mark the rhythm, whilst others danced and acted the episodes of the drama.

The opening chant described how Kipara tried to attract the attention of some women by his buffoonery. The antics of the excited Kipara were realistically portrayed by Tjalerina. Calling out in a loud, hoarse voice, he danced towards the singers with a curious hopping motion, his hips held stiffly, and feet close together, barely leaving the ground. At the climax, near the circle of chanting men, his cries became louder and more hoarse, and his actions so violent that he lost his balance, fell over backwards, and lay on the ground with his feet in the air, still roaring loudly. The men explained to me that Kipara's living descendant, the wild turkey[1] of today, still uses similar methods to attract the female bird during the mating season. He calls her with a deep, booming voice, and, when she approaches, becomes so

[1] *Eupodotis australis.*

agitated, and his actions so demonstrative, that often, like Kipara of old, he topples over.

Kipara's song for the blind Wood Pigeon formed the basis of the second act. One hot day, when the Wild Turkey was sitting in the shade of a mulga tree, his attention was attracted by a blind Wood Pigeon groping along the ground in search of water. The poor, famished creature was almost dead with thirst, for the spring on which it had lived had dried up during the hot weather.

Iputulita, kapi, wiara, niula, kana, wanmai,
softly chanted the men in rhythm with the helpless groping and plaintive cries of the perishing 'bird.' Slowly, inch by inch, it crept along, its face close to the ground and hands searching blindly from side to side, the very picture of helplessness and despair. Suddenly, as if by chance, the actor's hand fell into a hole (already dug and supposedly full of water). Instantly the tempo of the chanting quickened as the 'pigeon,' with an expression of intense joy, splashed his face, and drank noisily and greedily from the 'waterhole.'

In the next stage of the drama, which was acted to another chant composed by the Wild Turkey-man, two brown actors hopped about the ground, angrily stabbing at each other with sharp sticks. At some time in his wanderings, Kipara had released two of his spirit replicas, or *kuran*, from his body— all ancestral people had that power—so that they could go hunting for him. He was surprised and somewhat annoyed when, instead of doing as he wished, the Chicks, as they were called, quarrelled violently and attacked each other. The old man, after he had composed a song about the incident, reabsorbed the spirits into his body and continued his journey.

In the fourth act Kipara, impersonated by Tjalerina, had succeeded in stealing the fire-stick, and was on the alert against a surprise attack by his enemies. The actor was the very personification of stealth, vigilance and pure physical grace, as he sneaked in and out among the mulga trees, every step in time with the music, searching for enemies on the ground, around him, and in the skies above.

Niari, the half blind youth who had danced so well in the ceremony of the Mountain-devil, was the performer in the next act. He impersonated Wara, a small wallaby that had been disturbed by Kipara when having its morning meal of wild figs. The little creature, uncertain of Kipara, hopped to the crest of an adjacent ridge and watched him from the shelter of a low corkwood tree.

'Don't be afraid,' called out Kipara, 'I'm not a man, I won't hurt you. Come over here and we'll dance an *inma* (ceremony) together.'

'I can't,' replied Wara, the Wallaby, 'I don't know any songs, nor even how to paint myself.'

'Don't let that trouble you,' said the Wild Turkey, 'I'll make up the song, and,' he continued, taking a piece of bark from a nearby tree and wetting it with blood, 'you can wear this for *inma walka* (ceremonial marks).'

So Niara, wearing the decorations laid down by Kipara so long ago, mimed the actions of the nervous little wallaby as he hopped realistically from the group of low rocks to the plain beneath, pausing occasionally to lick himself, as all wallabies have done from those long distant times till now.

When the next act opened Kipara, with his fire-stick hidden in a tall chignon, was creeping stealthily among the trees collecting wild tomatoes for his evening meal. Suddenly he clasped his head and fell to the ground in agony. According to the myth, Kipara did not dare to lay the fire-stick on the ground while he was collecting food, for fear that his enemies might find it. So he bound it in his head-dress for safe keeping. But a wind, lately sprung up, fanned the glowing embers into a flame, and burned his head severely. Kipara's living descendants still wear a dark crown where their ancestor was scorched.

At the opening of the seventh act a number of players were endeavouring to persuade Kipara to return the fire-stick to its rightful owners. It appeared that the Wild Turkey-man, feeling lonely, had again released several of his spirit doubles, *kuran,* to dance an *inma* (ceremony) with him. Once more he was both surprised and annoyed when, instead of doing as he wished, his *kuran* tried to coax him to forgo his revenge. They persisted in their efforts until the old fellow, losing patience and pushing them aside, escaped into the bush, howling with rage.

In the finale, which followed almost immediately, the Wild Turkey-man was wandering aimlessly about with one fire-stick over his shoulder and another supposedly bound in his hair. Convinced by now that he had eluded his pursuers, Kipara was admiring his fire-stick and idly lighting the grass at his feet. In the low scrub, intent on the recapture of the stolen fire-stick, could be seen two Hawk-men creeping stealthily toward the old man. Kipara was unaware of his danger until, with a loud cry, the Hawk-men rushed in and tore the fire-stick from his head. The old villain died in agonies beside the circle of singers, for, according to the legend, his pursuers had torn out Kipara's brains when they wrenched the fire-stick away.

Although the ceremonies of the aborigines are possibly the most primitive form of drama, they resemble the great operas of Wagner in one important respect. Whereas he, by his incomparable media of music and acting, immortalized the mighty deeds of the gods and demi-gods of the ancient Nordic race, so, by their age-old chants and strange rituals, do the aborigines of today keep alive the epics of their heroic times.

But the function of these expressions in the two cultures is very different. To us they are a means of spending a pleasant evening, a diversion from the daily tasks; to the aborigines, the outward manifestations of their beliefs and philosophies.

The performance I had seen that afternoon was not play, it was a vital dramatic expression that linked the actors of the present with their ancestors of the dim and ghostly past. There was no applause, no admiring crowds, not even a few onlookers; each and every one was either chanting the songs or acting a part in one of their many dramas that lead back, by a hundred paths, to the mystic 'Dream Times' from which they sprang.

CHAPTER VI

The Medicine Man

OLD TJALERINA, THE CHIEF actor in the Wild Turkey ceremony, had always wanted to be a medicine man, but had not been able to reach the goal of his ambition. He told me that he had once been 'a little bit doctor,' able to hear the spirits at night time, though he could not see them. But he had lost even that power when, a few years previously, a serious illness had nearly cost him his life.

When he had recovered, he had given one 'doctor' many spears to rejuvenate him, but without success. From another he had purchased an australite (an obsidian button of meteoric origin), which, the second doctor man had assured Tjalerina, would make him an even bigger 'black-fella doctor' than before, if he succeeded in pushing the australite into his solar plexus. The poor old chap had tried to do that repeatedly, but in vain. In fact Tjalerina said his skin became so tender that he decided the extra power he would have gained was not worth the pain and trouble involved.

So, to cut his losses, he gave the australite to me, knowing that, as all giving in an aboriginal society is reciprocal, he at least would get something from me to offset his bad bargain.

He suggested at first that I might push the australite into my own body, but, on second thoughts, said that he did not think it was really necessary; I was already a 'big fella doctor' because I could make a box (wireless) talk. Nevertheless, he added, an australite might help me to do other wonderful things. Knowing my limitations in those matters —I had not learned conjuring—I thanked the old man, gave him an ample present of food, and suggested that, if he would tell me about the magic stone, I would prefer to take it back to my own country to show it to other 'white fella doctors' even more powerful than myself.

41

I learned from Tjalerina that australites are the special property of their *nungari* (medicine men), just as quartz crystals are the stock-in-trade of the aboriginal doctors of the southern tribes. Those meteoric stones have many functions in the hands of the *nungari*. They will restore his failing powers if inserted into his body, and act as a watch-dog over his property when he is absent. They will also tell him the direction of an enemy, and assist him when performing healing rites on his fellow tribesmen.

There was a young blind medicine man, Nemienya, in our camp, who was reputed to be both skilled and powerful. I was surprised that so young a man, particularly as he was afflicted with blindness, should be in the possession of secrets, which I had thought belonged to the aged. But I was mistaken. Any youth showing unusual personality, and more than ordinary interest in tribal lore and the psychic doings of the medicine men, was looked upon by the elders as a possible future member of the medical profession. The youth, however, would be totally unaware of their interest, and, without knowing, would have to pass strange tests before the secrets of the medicine men were imparted to him.

Apparently Nemienya, the blind man, not only possessed the necessary psychic qualifications, but had stood up to the tests, for already he had been initiated and trained in the mysteries and practices of a *nungari* by Wilu, his tribal father, himself a noted medicine man.

When Nemienya was sufficiently mature to be trusted with that secret knowledge, Wilu had taken his spirit, under the cover of night, to the distant land of the *nungari*, which lies far south of the Pitjendadjara country, to show him its many dark and cryptic mysteries.

But before Wilu could make that journey, his spirit had to undergo a remarkable transformation. It left its human body by the fireside and changed, first into the shape of an eagle-hawk, then turned itself entirely inside out by thrusting its head through its vent from the inside. This metamorphosis placed the feathers on the inside of the body, made the wings into legs, and, conversely, the legs into wings. It was only in this curiously inverted form that Wilu could take the spirit of Nemienya from his sleeping body, and carry it to the summit of a high pillar of rock in that strange land of the medicine men, the *nungari*.

From that high place, the *kuran* (spirit) of Wilu pointed out and explained to Nemienya the wonders and secrets of that extraordinary world; the pool of blood, always kept covered with branches by the spirits of the *nungari*; the kurrajong tree, whose bright green leaves had been replaced by the feathers of desert birds; as well as many other strange sights of which I could learn but little. Few, if any, white men have been admitted into the occult and psychic world of the medicine men.

Before dawn both Wilu and Nemienya returned to their empty bodies by the fireside, for it was only safe for their dis-embodied spirits to be abroad in the darkness. Nemienya's spirit entered his body without difficulty, for it had not altered its shape. But the spirit of old Wilu, being still in the likeness of an inverted eagle-hawk, had to change itself back, first into the ordinary bird, then into the likeness of a man, before it could re-enter his sleeping body.

The morning following that adventure, Wilu would have enquired casually of Nemienya:

'What did you dream last night?'

If Nemienya had no memory of his experience, or had dreamt of other things, the doctor would have asked no other questions, for the answers themselves would have shown that his pupil was not ready for fuller instruction. Again, at some later time, the spirit of Wilu would have to transform itself into the inverted eagle-hawk, and take his relative, Nemienya, on that long, strange journey. If then Nemienya had remembered the experience, the old man would have proceeded with further instruction; if not, the journey would still have to be repeated.

The aborigines round my fireside said that it was quite possible that many of them had made that journey, but they could not recall it, although Jabiaba thought he could remember 'little fella bit.' Indeed, scarcely any aborigines recollect that journey; those who do so are the fortunate ones, for to be a medicine man is the high honour which all desire but few attain.

By the time Nemienya had completed his training, he was conversant with not only the arts of healing, by magic, but also the means of controlling the dangerous spirits of darkness. However, to practise his magic he, like Wilu, had to change himself into an inverted eagle-hawk before he could see the *mamu*, a tree-dwelling demon that attacks the aboriginal's spirits at night; foil the souls of the lonely dead in their attempts to capture those of the living; and guide the snowy-haired *julanya*, the childish sprites who are always searching for earthly mothers.

The *mamu* is especially feared, for it is always on the look-out for the *kuran* (spirits) of little children who have left their sleeping bodies and, heedless of the dangers of the night, frolic among the gum trees. Sometimes the *mamu* succeeds in catching one of those little sprites as a meal for itself and its ghoulish companions. Should this happen, the child, now bereft of its *kuran*, will be listless and out of sorts in the morning. If Nemienya, or any other medicine man, knows of the sickness in time, he can save the child's life by taking its little spirit from the *mamu*, and placing it in the body of the child, for the *mamu* does not eat the victim immediately, but plays with it, just like a cat with a mouse. However, the *mamu* is cunning, and if the medicine man is not close to it before he attacks the *mamu* will eat the little spirit, and the child will die.

The aborigines do not understand that disease and death take their rise from natural causes. They believe that these afflictions are the result of the evil magic of some ancestral forebear or evil person, and can only be cured by the counter magic of the medicine man.

Several times we heard of the healing powers of Nemienya, and his control over the evil spirits, but did not come into personal contact with him until Moanya strained his back bringing in a heavy log of wood. Knowing that Moanya would have a strange story to tell, I asked him what was the cause of the pain in his back.

". . . a young, blind medicine-man, Nemienya, . . . who was reputed to be both skilled and powerful." *(Page 42.)*

"Knowing that Moanya would have a strange story to tell . . . ."   (Page 44.)

It seemed that this was not the first attack. Several years previously Moanya and his wife, Numidi, when living in their tribal country in the Mann Ranges, having dug out a large number of rabbits on a particularly hot day, went to sleep in the shade of a desert oak. Later, when they were preparing a fire to cook the rabbits, Moanya was seized with such violent pains in his back that he had a difficulty in reaching the main camp. That evening the pains became so severe that his agonized cries awakened the whole camp. Quickly Numidi and some of the men lit a fire, covered it with a thick layer of eucalyptus leaves, and laid the groaning man on the top. That primitive application of heat, after all one of the best cures for lumbago, soon eased the pain and the sufferer went to sleep.

The following day a medicine man was called in. After much enquiry and deliberation he decided that Wambina, a mythical man who had created that part of the country, had speared Moanya in the back with a *kulpidji* (sacred stick) because he had caught too many rabbits at one time. By dint of much magic, rubbing, and the sucking of the painful spot, the medicine man extracted most of the stick from Moanya's back, and, for the time being, the patient recovered. Moanya told us, however, he felt sure that some of the fragments of the *kulpidji* still remained, for they often troubled him. He intended to ask Nemienya, the blind medicine man, to take them out on the following day.

I waited until the operation was well under way before going across to see what was happening. Moanya was resting on his hands and knees in the sand, while Nemienya energetically squeezed and massaged the flesh and skin around the lumbar region. Every now and again the doctor extracted a fragment of the offending stick, and, carrying it in his cupped hands, turned his back on the patient and allowed the splinter to 'fly' away. However, as all the splinters could not be extracted by massage, Nemienya sucked vigorously at the painful spot for some time before he finally extracted the last and largest of the missing fragments of the *kulpidji* (sacred stick).

When Moanya returned to our camp he claimed that he was entirely cured, and indeed it seemed so, for during the whole four months that he was with us he showed no further signs of pain in his back.

'Will you give Nemienya anything for making your back good-fella?' I asked Moanya.

'P'raps,' said the aboriginal casually, 'or him give me 'notha big fella pain alonga back.'

'But,' he added, 'me got nothing' now, one fella spear, no more.'

Which was true enough, for only a few days previously I had inadvertently walked on his only spear-thrower.

Following the healing of Moanya, I often watched the medicine man at his craft. His methods were nearly always the same. He would massage the painful spot, taking up the flesh in handfuls, and then pretend to extract a stick or a piece of bark, always under the cover of one hand. Sometimes he would pass the stick, which was usually nothing more than a piece of bark or twig, to the admiring bystanders; at other times he would turn his back and allow it to 'fly' away.

But on one occasion he adopted an entirely different technique. A young woman, who worked for Mrs. Ward, became ill with a violent headache. Her mistress, with her usual kindliness towards those folk, gave the girl aspros and other drugs, but without effect. The girl begged to be allowed to go to her own camp, and once there, Nemienya was called in. He listened to the excited explanations with truly professional gravity (I have seen the same expression at my own bedside), then, without even a remark, solemnly, with his finger tips, felt the patient's head all over, and announced that it was cracked right down the middle.

I know that his diagnosis would not be accepted in our medical world, but I admired his simile. There have been occasions when, if a medical man had told me that my skull was cleft from crown to base and opening and shutting continuously, I would have believed him without question.

After the examination, Nemienya, taking the girl's head

between his hands, pressed it together several times, until he was satisfied that the crack was closed.

For the time being the patient recovered and went to sleep. But during the night she became worse, and early in the morning her parents, without calling the medicine man, smoked her over a fire (similar to the method used on Moanya). She endured that treatment for a few minutes, then suddenly fainted. There was an excited rush for blind Nemienya. But, like all his kind, refusing to be hurried, he strolled leisurely across, guided by the commotion round the camp fire of the sick girl.

For a while he did nothing. Then, dropping on his knees, he began to search frantically in the breakwind, behind which the sick girl was lying, for something invisible to the onlookers. After several unsuccessful attempts, Nemienya captured it in his cupped hands. Motioning the parents to turn the patient on her back, he pressed his hands firmly against her abdomen, holding them in that position for several seconds. The young woman returned to consciousness, and later to good health.

The doctor explained that the smoking had so frightened her *kuran* (spirit) that it had escaped from her body and sought refuge in the windbreak of boughs. The little spirit had been most difficult to catch, for it was very nervous and upset by the treatment it had received. The situation had been serious, for, if he, the doctor, had not been successful, the girl would have died, for no one can live long without their *kuran*.

It was fairly certain that, in that tribe at least, the medicine man was not feared to any extent, if at all. On the other hand he appeared to be a very busy person. He had to guard the camp from the unwelcome attentions of the dead, rescue the living from the clutches of the *mamu*, watch for spirit children on their search for earthly mothers, and cure the various ills of the community.

He should have received payment for his services, but no doubt, like all of his kind, both primitive and modern, he had a great deal of trouble in collecting his fees.

Chapter VII

Arrangements for the Desert Journey

WE HAD, BY NOW, SPENT almost a month at Ernabella, and were getting ready for the extended journey through the Central Aboriginal Reserves in company with a number of native informants.

Those reserves, which include portions of the desert country in South, Central and Western Australia, are the last strongholds of the aborigines in the southern parts of the continent, and have been set apart for their exclusive use. Theoretically they can live there unmolested and unharmed, for, according to the law, none but accredited scientists and officials are allowed access. In actual fact, as later events proved, that was far from being the true situation.

The Central Aboriginal Reserves all lie within a low rainfall area, and consist of extensive arid, sandy deserts, broken by the bare rocky mountain chains of the Musgrave, Petermann and Mann Ranges, and the lesser Tomkinson and Rawlinson groups.

The rocky slopes of the ranges are almost devoid of earth, and support little more than the ubiquitous spinifex (*Trioda* sp.), a limited flora of native pines (*Callitris* sp.), stunted corkwoods (*Hakea* sp.) and the various desert acacias. The flats, within and on the outskirts of the ranges, are remarkably level, and, in some places, are even without watercourses, for the amount of rain that falls on the adjacent hillsides is often so small that it is absorbed before it reaches the plains.

The Musgrave Ranges are by far the largest and finest in the whole reserve. With its outliers, the Ayers Range, it is approximately one hundred and fifty miles long, and rises, at Mt. Woodroffe, to over four thousand feet, possibly the highest in South Australia. The other ranges are neither as extensive nor have they the elevation of the Musgraves.

48

"... for she (Numidi) was the brightest and most willing of the aboriginal women ...." *(Page 56.)*

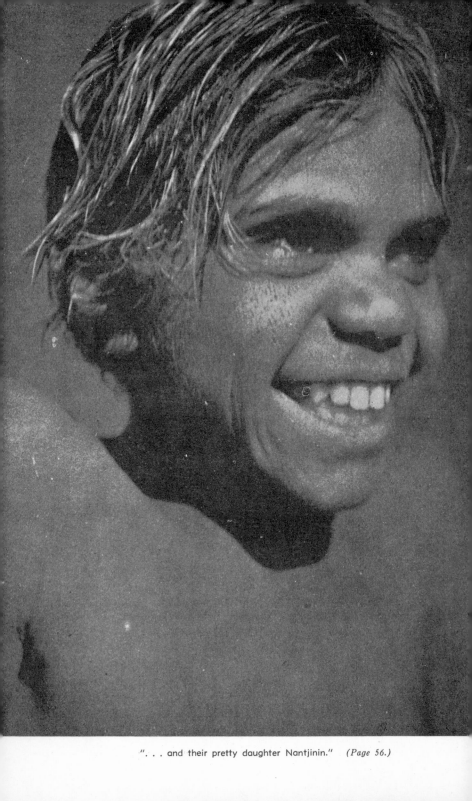

"... and their pretty daughter Nantjinin." *(Page 56.)*

From the north, south, east and west, the desert surrounds the ranges like an encircling sea. But in spite of the fact that it is a true desert, and devoid of surface waters, it is not by any means the waste of bare, drifting sandhills that most people suppose. Much of the region consists of flats that carry a variety of drought-resisting plants and trees, which, after good rain, are made gay with the profuse purple-flowering parakeelia (*Calandrinia balonnensis*) and other desert plants.

The sandhill country, on the other hand, consists of either jumbled hillocks or parallel lines of dunes that 'march' in the direction of their length, which is the same as that of the prevailing wind. Those sand dunes, which, I understand, are peculiar to Australia, are often so regular that, when seen from the air, they resemble a gigantic plowed field. Although the sand ridges have a drifting crest, the sides are vegetated with a sparse desert flora that has adjusted itself to its arid environment, while the swales between are often filled with either dense thickets of mulga (*Acacia aneura*) or the melancholy, but graceful, desert oak (*Casuarina descaineana*).

The lands of the Pitjendadjara tribe are situated in and around the Mann Range, which lies astride the borders of South, Central and Western Australia. This range is a low, granitic chain, which, towards the west, first breaks down into isolated hills, and then, finally, is engulfed in the surrounding desert.

In my original scheme, we had planned to take the scientific equipment, with three months' supply of food, and make a wide circuit, north-east through Mt. Conner, Ayers Rock, Mt. Olga, across the desert to the Petermanns, thence to the Warburton Ranges, where we hoped to continue my previous research. From there we intended to return to the starting point through the Mann and Musgrave Ranges.

But when we saw the condition of Tjundaga's string, made up as it was of old, decrepit camels and colts that had not carried a load, we began to doubt the wisdom of the original scheme. The saddles, camel boxes and gear were also in a

E

bad state, even though Tjundaga and Nibiana had spent
many hours patching and repairing them. To make matters
worse, the short-wave transmitting set, which the Mission
folk were lending us, refused to function, in spite of much
shouting into its microphone, many conferences, and communal investigations of its internal organs. The last misfortune meant that, after leaving Lindavale, only about four
days out, we would be entirely cut off from civilization.
It was obvious, then, that with doubtful means of transport, and none of communication after the first few days,
such a journey would be unnecessarily risky, even though
Tjundaga's beasts were looking better after their month's
rest; and the loan of several camels from the superintendent
of the Mission had further increased the reliability of the
string.

So we decided to forgo our visit to the Petermann and
Warburton Ranges, and split the remainder of the original
route into two sections; the first to cover Mt. Conner, Ayers
Rock, Mt. Olga, then back to Ernabella; the second, after
reloading supplies, to head west along the Musgraves, then
on to the Mann Ranges, which we had learned would be an
important centre of research. The re-arranged plans would
still give us plenty of opportunities for investigation and
put much less strain on the camel string.

Our string was made up of dromedaries—ungainly one-
humped beasts, the progeny of the original stock from
Arabia—which were especially suited for the long, waterless
stages that stretched ahead of us. Tjundaga had already
hardened them, that is, trained them to go without water
for long periods, so we could travel them safely for five or
more days in dry country, and much longer if there was an
abundance of young green herbage. Nor would their food
have to be carried, for camels can live, and actually fatten,
on the wire-like leaves of mulga and the low-growing
acacias. These fodder trees are common, in fact, on previous
expeditions in those parts, I do not remember any night
camp that did not have an abundance of food for the beasts.

There were four types of camels in our string. The riding camels, slightly built, had been chosen for their easy gait. Then there were the water and box camels, the former to carry our precious water supply of four eight-gallon drums, and the latter, two large boxes, in which were stored the valuable scientific equipment, cameras, and immediate food requirements. The pack camels, sturdy beasts, would bear the less perishable goods, boxes of groceries, tents, tarpaulins and other impedimenta, while the more or less unbroken colts would be given the flour and sugar loads, which could not be damaged even if the youngsters decided to bolt.

It was imperative that both the box and water camels should be quiet and reliable, for on them depended not only the success of our research, but our lives, as it is not unusual for a restive camel to break out of the string without warning and gallop wildly over the countryside, bucking off its load as it goes. Should the water camel run amok in the middle of a dry stage, some of which are a hundred miles long, it would be a calamity of the first magnitude. So, without knowing it, and, by her supercilious appearance, not caring if she did, that beast literally carried our lives on her back. However, Tjundaga assured us that 'she was properly quiet fella,' and events proved he was right.

The method of loading a pack camel is unusual. A double saddle, which fits over the hump, is held in place by two straps, one round the neck and another under the tail. These prevent the load from slipping backward, when going uphill, or forward on the downgrade. As there is no surcingle to keep the saddle in a central position, that is accomplished by arranging the load so that there is an equal weight on either side. Such adjustment, particularly with heterogeneous gear, calls for some skill; in fact, the ability of a camel man is judged by the frequency or otherwise with which he has to stop the string to adjust his saddles.

A camel is guided in a different manner from a horse. One end of a light line, usually made of whip-cord, is attached to a stud-like nose-peg, which projects through an artificial slit in the nostril, the other end to a length of rope which is tied to the next beast in front. In case of an accident, or if the creature is restive, the nose-line will break, and prevent the nostril of the camel from being injured. But if the camel is used for riding, a pair of light lines, tied to the nose-peg, takes the place of the familiar reins and bridle. The riding saddles are of a different construction and much lighter than those used for the packs. They fit over the hump in the same manner, but are held down with a surcingle. They have two sections, one in front, and one held behind the hump. On the front section is piled the bedding, water bags, and small articles, while on the rear sits the rider, almost over the animal's tail, in a picturesque and not uncomfortable position.

The action of the camel is a series of short, gentle lunges, by no means unpleasant and, once one becomes accustomed to the movement, no more tiring than the action of a horse.

But to a beginner dismounting is apt to be a little frightening. Should a rider wish to leave his elevated position for a more stable environment, he calls the magic word 'Hooshta.' With no more ado the creature drops forward on its knees, with a jolt that threatens to project the rider into space. Just as that calamity seems about to happen, the action goes into reverse as the beast settles on its haunches, shuffles backwards and forwards for a few times, then comes to rest. Mounting is the same series of movements in the opposite sequence.

Although camels will carry their heavy loads, day after day, without apparent effort, they only do so under continual protest, for they are surely one of the most vocal and unhappy of creatures. It is seldom that there is not some beast in the string moaning or roaring over some fancied grievance. My mount, an ancient, disgruntled cow, even started to cry before I placed the saddle on her back, and the mere action of tightening the surcingle called for a burst of sound that would have stirred any man's heart to compassion—if he did not know camels.

The slow pace of a camel, a steady three miles an hour, though most irritating when one is in a hurry, was a decided

"In front of it was the most beautiful corkwood tree I have ever seen." *(Page 63.)*

". . . in the background flat-topped Mt. Conner, its red precipices lit by the mellow sun of late afternoon." *(Page 63.)*

advantage for our research, for at that speed the aborigines could follow us comfortably, and, when necessary, I could walk with them to discuss aspects of their life, or gather the legendary stories of some place we happened to pass.

We wanted a few aboriginal families to travel with us so that we could observe their daily actions and their relationships to each other, for by those observations, small in themselves, we would be able to gain a fuller insight into certain aspects of their society. So, from among the many applicants, for there was no shortage of volunteers, we finally chose two families—Tjalerina, the chief actor in the Wild Turkey ceremony, Jundin, his wife, and their little son, Naniwanya; Moanya, the aborigine whose lumbago was cured by the medicine man, Numidi, his wife, and their pretty daughter, Nantjinin, about eleven years old.

A few evenings before our departure, however, there was an incident which bid fair to alter the plans of our expedition. While we were having tea with Mrs. Ward we heard a great noise of shouting and screaming in the native camp. Mr. Ward, Lauri and I rushed across and found the whole place in an uproar. Angry men were standing round their brightly burning fires, spears and spearthrowers in hand and eyes flashing in the firelight; women, their shrill voices raised in expostulation and anger; and crying children everywhere. Just outside Tjundaga's camel camp we saw a ring of excited, chattering women, and, in the middle of them, stiff and insensible, was the newly chosen member of our party, Numidi. She had been hit, and nobody seemed to know why, by one of the quietest and kindliest aborigines in the camp. We tried to pour sal volatile down her throat, but her teeth were so tightly clenched that I could not open them, even with a wedge of wood. Moanya, her husband, however, quickly summing up the situation, seized Numidi's upper jaw in one hand, her chin in the other, and, with a quick wrench, opened her mouth sufficiently for us to pour down a dose of restorative.

Some time elapsed before it took effect, then, without warning, her senses returned. All the pent-up rage that was about to be expressed when the stunning blow prevented further action, flared up again. With her eyes still glassy, and hardly able to stand, she grabbed a glowing stick, and, brandishing it, staggered off to punish her unknown enemy. She struggled for a while with the women who tried to quieten her, but finally gave in and sat down by the fire. ·

Suddenly another paroxysm of rage overcame her. Unable to get up because of the women round her, she gave vent to her feelings in a series of high-pitched, hysterical screams, punctuated by the low, moaning sound of a death chant, which, the men said, somewhat fearfully, would be effective if only Numidi knew the name of her assailant. Rapidly, as she chanted, the half-crazed woman pushed her bare feet backwards and forwards over the glowing coals, totally oblivious of the heat, so obsessed was she with her incantations. She then turned round and screamed to us to go home and stop interfering in 'blackfella' business.

We knew her remark was true enough in its way, but we also knew that Numidi's abusive tongue would soon stir up the fight afresh should we obey her orders; so to prevent further trouble we administered a heavy dose of bromide and carried her to her camp, where she continued, in a low voice, to tell her unknown adversary about his parentage, his past deeds and future punishments.

By the time we went to bed, all the natives had returned to their camps; the fires had died down and quiet reigned over the lately disturbed people. By the morning, the animosity of both Numidi and those who took part in the quarrel would be forgotten, for the aborigines do not seem to bear any malice once the trouble is over.

The day following, I heard the full story behind the disturbance. Just as we were preparing the evening meal, a young boy, Inakinya, had tried to look into my tent, and his father, no doubt considering it to be an act of discourtesy, had forbidden him to do so. This unaccustomed restriction so annoyed the boy that he lost his temper, and threw stones toward a group of old men with whom his father was sitting. But no one in the group took any action against the boy for

his attack; they simply laughed at him. The father, thinking the trouble would blow over if he took the boy away,
walked towards his camp and called the boy to follow. The
lad, still smarting under the restriction and ridicule to which
he had been subjected, not only ignored the order, but
picked up a ten-foot hunting spear and, with considerable
skill, threw it at his father.

Everyone in the camp, men, women and children, thought
that the display of temper was the best of jokes and laughed
uproariously. The lad, unable to vent his rage on anyone,
helpless and bewildered by the ridicule and laughter, gave
up the fight, threw himself down on the sand and howled
his heart out from sheer futility.

That evening, when the matter was being discussed,
Jabiaba said to the father in the native tongue:

'Why don't you stop your son from behaving like that in
front of the white people?'

Tilbukuna, the father, instantly took umbrage at the
remark.

'What business is it of yours, Pukita (childless man)?
My boy is no worse than any other.'

Jabiaba replied smartly, for he was sensitive over the
inference. Both men lost their tempers and were soon
brandishing spears and shouting threats at each other. The
counsel of others, however, prevailed, and the disagreement
temporarily died down. Then one of the women, a well-
known mischief maker, started to sing a song disparaging
Tilbukuna. He threatened the woman. Her husband,
Numidi's brother, intervened, and the fight was on again.
Numidi rushed across to help her brother, but was stopped
by a back-hand blow from a quiet old aborigine who wanted
to keep her out of the row. Unfortunately, he either hit
her on the chin or on the back of the head, for the next they
knew, Numidi was lying insensible on the ground, and we
white folk were coming to see what was the cause of the
trouble.

In the morning we went to see Numidi, who was certainly
a sick woman. Although she accepted a few sweets, she

showed no other interest in life, a contrast indeed to her usual conduct, for she was easily the brightest and most willing of all the aboriginal women in the camp.

Within a few days my wife left for civilization, for one must have either previous knowledge or youth to endure the strain of the long desert journeys.

Then came the final rush. Our camp had to be dismantled and everything arranged for the loads. Essentials had to be sorted from non-essentials, safe places found for the scientific equipment, the cameras and medical supplies, and a hundred and one other things had to receive attention.

It was surprising how long it took to get the camel string under way on the last day. Just as we were ready, a load would have to be adjusted, Nibiana would go away to say good-bye to yet another of her friends, or one of the staff would be missing. Finally, late in the afternoon, we succeeded, and moved off accompanied by most of the aborigines and dogs in the camp. After several miles I had to send the natives back, for otherwise we would not have had sufficient food to last the journey, or water in the canteens to carry us over the dry stages.

The final party consisted of Tjundaga, Nibiana, and a little girl, Kitata, who helped with the camels; Tjalerina, the old actor, with his wife and child; Moanya and Numidi, who insisted on coming in spite of her injuries, with their daughter; Tjikaba, an old Ernabella man going to Lyndavale; Lauri and myself; twelve human beings, and twelve camels.

As we expected, the string did not travel well. Tjundaga's camels and those of the Mission were not used to each other; the colts were trying to throw their loads, and several of the packs were out of balance.

We camped that night on a level plain, carpeted with the flaxen-white mulga grass and surrounded by rugged russet-coloured hills. Sleep came slowly. Perhaps I was wondering what was ahead of me, or perhaps I was only cold, for when I woke in the morning both Lauri's sleeping bag and my own were covered with a thick layer of frost.

CHAPTER VIII

The Journey to Lyndavale

OUR FIRST STOP, SO TO SPEAK, was Lyndavale, a station on the outskirts of civilization some seventy miles from Ernabella. We had made arrangements with 'Snowy' Pearce, the owner, to pick up, at his station, a native who belonged to Ayers Rock country, for one of the objects of the north-easterly journey was to establish a camp at the Rock, and collect its legends, as well as sketch and photograph the many aboriginal paintings in the caves at its base.

Excepting for the first day in the Musgrave Ranges, the journey to Lyndavale was through low mulga scrub, which, even from the back of the camel, limited our view to within a few yards on either side of the track. As our surroundings varied but little from one part of the day to another, that journey was possibly the most monotonous of the whole of the expedition. Yet, in spite of that, I found much to interest me, for I had lived with the aborigines long enough to have learned that the surface of the ground has always a story to tell. It is like a great book, from the pages of which the initiated can read the daily events of bushland, the comings and goings of the birds and animals, and the industry of the lowlier creatures. Even with my untrained eyes and mind I missed but few of the tracks of the kangaroos, emus, mallee hens, and a host of small reptiles that crossed our path.

The homes of the desert insects were a succession of surprises. There is a spider—I wonder if it is known to the scientific world—which, as it digs its home, a vertical hole in the sandy soil, coats each load of earth brought to the surface with a light, silken web, and then deposits the load on the circumference of a circle about eight inches from the entrance. There is also an allied spider which places its little dumps of coated sand in a neat pile on one side of its nest.

The natives consider both these insects dangerous, and call them *inba kuran kuran,* which translated literally means 'the spider that sucks the life (*kuran*) from its victims.'

I also saw many homes of the curious mulga ant, an insect which builds a mud wall, up to fourteen inches in diameter and five inches in height, round the mouth of its nest, and then thatches the wall with dead mulga leaves. There were nests in all stages of construction, first only the bare mud walls, then with a few leaves in position, and the ground nearby covered with thousands which the workers had pulled in during the hours of darkness, and, and finally, the completed nests, entirely thatched with mulga leaves.

In the warm weather there is a tiny ant, not as large as a grain of sugar, which is the bane of all travellers, brown or white. The ants seem to know by some uncanny instinct when human beings are about, for hardly did we stop near one of their nests than a line of them formed up and came towards us. They attack those parts of the body that are moist with perspiration, such as between the fingers, under the arms, and other uncomfortable places. Their bite is like the sting of a wasp, a most distressing insect, and responsible for an inordinate amount of bad language. The aborigines, when they are in 'ant' country, keep the pests at bay by a ring of small fires, which appears to be the only efficient protection.

Just before reaching Lyndavale we passed a place where a lowan or mallee hen (*Leipoa ocellata*) had neatly scratched a hollow in the ground for a nest, and already had a layer of leaves in place. It was a surprisingly large hole, about ten feet across, and almost two feet deep, a worthy effort for two birds scarcely larger than a domestic fowl. As the season advanced the birds would continue to scratch sand and leaves into the centre, until they had made a mound that would be well above ground level. In that the eggs would be placed in circles, usually in three layers. The heat from the rotting vegetation, coupled with the habit of the birds of opening out the top of the mound on sunny days, would provide the necessary warmth for incubation.

Several times I noticed deep holes under the trees, with a rough shelter on top. Those, old Tjalerina told me, were places where the natives, when journeying between the Musgrave Ranges and Lyndavale, had buried themselves during the heat of the day. He further explained that when aborigines are forced to travel in summer over long, dry stages, they do not set out on their journey until nightfall. Before leaving the last waterhole, they drink as much as possible, then keep going until a little after sunrise. When the day starts to warm up, the aborigines dig a hole under a tree until they reach the cool sand. Then they put a rough shelter over the top, reduce their skin temperature by throwing sand over their bodies, bury themselves up to the neck, and remain covered until the cool of the evening allows them to continue their way.

It has been contended that the aborigines are able to make such journeys, impossible to white men, because they are better equipped by nature for such tasks. But it is likely, however, that the theorists are wrong, and that the holes under the trees provide the real answer. That simple, yet wise, method of defeating the elements suggests that the aborigines, by purely empirical means, had discovered that the length of time that a man can live without water is governed by the rate of his body moisture, and to prevent that vital loss they travel only at night, burying themselves by day. It would seem, then, that the capacity to make those exhausting journeys is not a matter of the aborigines being better equipped than the Europeans, but rather that they have used a little more intelligence in dealing with a difficult problem. Many a white man need not have perished had he adopted so simple an expedient.

The camel string was much slower than we expected. What with late starts, restive colts, and broken nose-lines, it was almost five days before we plodded our weary way into the station at Lyndavale. I was disappointed to find that 'Snowy' Pearce, the owner, was not at home, nor, by the tracks, had anyone been near the station for some days. However, at Maratjara waterhole, about a mile from the station, we saw indications that a man on horseback had been there only a few hours previously. Before we made camp that evening I asked old Tjalerina to follow those tracks, and, if they led to the camp of a white man, to let him know that we had arrived.

It was late next morning before the old man came back with the news that 'Snowy' Pearce was away, but that Charlie Lester, his assistant, was looking after the sheep about five miles north, and wanted Lauri and me to visit him.

Charlie was preparing a meal when we reached his camp, wild turkey roasting in a camp-oven, which, with true bush hospitality, he insisted on sharing. And while we ate he told of that nearest to his heart, his half-caste daughter, Milly, who was living at a church home in Melbourne.

'She's a wonderful girl,' said Charlie, as he produced a much-fingered snapshot, 'she writes to me every week. Wants me to give up smoking and drinking, because they're no good. I've managed the booze alright, but this smoking business has got me beat. I put the old pipe away, and I'm all right when I'm by myself, but as soon as 'Snowy' comes along with his stink-pot I'm gone. Still, I'll do my best, because I'd like to be able to please Milly.'

Tenderly and with great pride he produced her letters— by their grimy appearance, read and re-read many times —faded eyes alight, and his fingers trembling as he pointed out the treasured passages. He was a rough, old bushman, untidy and unkempt, and somewhat the butt of the country-side. He might almost have been classed as one of life's failures, had it not been for the bright, shining star that had led him on to supreme endeavour. All the money he could save went to his daughter for her education. It was little enough, but it was his all. And I think, by what I saw in that battered photograph, his ideal was worthy of the sacrifice.

We returned to camp with the Ayers Rock man, filled the canteens, and were just ready to move off, when over the hill came 'Snowy' Pearce.

'By jove, old man,' he said, 'I was afraid I was going to miss you. The abos saw your smokes yesterday.' (We had

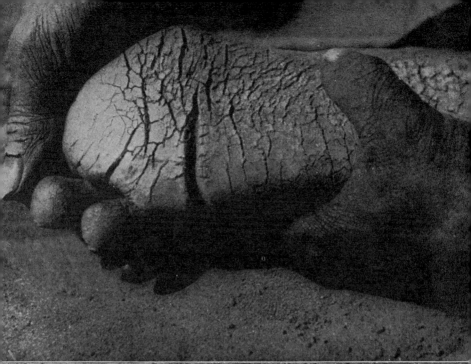

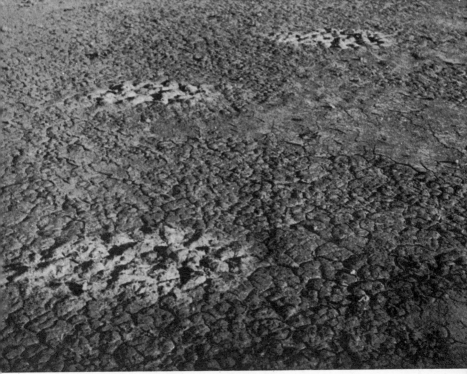

THE LEGEND OF THE ICE-MEN OF MT. CONNER

(a) "It is one of the aboriginal beliefs that the deep cracks across the soles of their feet . . . are made by the ice left behind in the grass by the Ninya (Ice) men." *(Page 64.)*

(b) "The icy blood that pours from the wounds . . . are now large, white—not red—patches on the claypan floor." *(Page 64.)*

"The journey from Mt. Conner to Ayers Rock led us across sixty miles of arid, trackless desert of sand-dunes."   (Page 71.)

been lighting spinifex to herald our arrival.) 'But I couldn't get in any sooner.'

'What!' he exclaimed, when he saw the camel-string already loaded, 'you're surely not going out this afternoon. Good God, I haven't spoken to anyone but Charlie, or the blackfellows, for weeks.'

'Get up on the lorry,' he added almost beseechingly, 'and send the string along to my camp. I can't let you go like this.'

We could ill-afford another day, but I too had known the loneliness of the bush; so, without demur, I motioned the camel-string to follow, and Lauri and I climbed aboard.

What an evening we had! Our conversation covered all fields: the success of 'Snowy's' station; the doings of our mutual acquaintances, for 'Snowy' and I had met some years previously; and, because Lauri's little portable receiver brought them the first news they had heard for months, a discussion on the international situation. Then I remember Lauri picking up a broadcast of a church service in Melbourne, and Charlie's shy request that we listen-in for a while.

'I wonder if my girl is there?' he said, his wistful eyes gazing into the fire. 'She goes to church every Sunday.'

After that, Gladys Moncrieff sang 'Land of Hope and Glory.' Little did I realize, as I listened to the liquid notes of the singer, expressing the love for our country much more fully than the spoken word, and watched the faces of my companions in the fitful light of the fire, that ere two years would pass I would be the only one left of that little group. Both 'Snowy' and Charlie had passed to the Great Beyond before I heard of them again, and Lauri had given his gallant young life in the defence of all we hold most dear.

Chapter IX

Mt. Conner and the Ice Men

We said good-bye to the two bushmen next morning, both fine men, although so totally different. 'Snowy' had treated his native wife with all the generosity that Charlie had accorded his daughter.

'Snowy' had been doubtful whether the soaks at Mt. Conner would yield enough water to carry us across the desert to Ayers Rock, and indeed it seemed, at least for the first two days, that he was right. Amarari soak, which we reached on the sunset of the first day, was practically dry. The aborigines had followed the dwindling water supplies down through the sand for almost twelve feet, and although we allowed the water to collect all night, there were only about two gallons the next morning. Near noon, the following day, we were taken to a rock cavity containing a good two hundred gallons of clear water, but, to our disappointment, found it far too salt to drink. It was late on the same afternoon that we located Anneri soak, a hole about six feet across, situated in the middle of an extensive clay-pan.

It is small wonder that travellers without native helpers, or a knowledge of Australian bush-craft, die of thirst in that country. Water-holes, such as Anneri, are almost impossible to find, except where experience has taught the significance of the faint game-pad, or the flight of the diamond-sparrows.

Anneri soak, on inspection, showed only a small puddle of water, so small indeed that Lauri and I decided that the shortage of water had ruined our chance of reaching Ayers Rock from the easterly direction. But Matinya, the new helper from Lyndavale, revived our sinking spirits by announcing that there was *kapi-bulka* (water large), and the soak only required cleaning out to give us all that we required. We left the native men to do the work, and moved on toward Mt. Conner, where we intended to camp for several days.

Up till then, the mulga scrub and low trees on the rough, stony hills had allowed only an occasional glimpse of the mountain, but as we approached from the south-west, where the plain extends to its base, I was able to see the mountain in its entirety for the first time. It was a scene that one does not easily forget. In the foreground were the sand-dunes, rich with lovely colours; red sand, flaxen-white spinifex, dark-green and glossy *Duboisia hopwoodii*, the dreaded camel poison, and smoky-grey saltbush; in the background, flat-topped Mt. Conner, its red precipices lit by the mellow sun of late afternoon.

We reached the foot of the mountain and pitched our camp by the light of a brilliant sunset, our tents rosy-red and the cliffs above glowing as living coals against a sky the colour of a galah's breast.

I spent the next morning wandering by myself at the base of the mount, once a part of that lofty rampart now scattered on all sides. At the time, I felt a mere dwarf amid such greatness; yet, in retrospect, what I remembered most was not the towering cliffs, nor the gigantic boulders, but the delicate colouring of the hillsides, carpeted as they were with myriads of stones, buff, yellow and creamy-white, and spotted with misty-grey desert plants, bunches of golden-yellow grass and spinifex.

One simple piece of scenery was as exquisite as an ancient Chinese print. A large honey-coloured cliff, fully lit by the mid-morning sun, overhung the valley. In the front of it was the most beautiful corkwood tree I have ever seen. Its roots were buried in yellow spinifex and red stones, and its branches backed by an azure-blue sky. The cliff, the sky, the lovely tree, with its dark trunk, strangely twisted limbs and grey, pendulous foliage, made as decorative a picture as any Oriental artist could have conceived.

I returned to camp with the beauty of the surroundings still strong in my mind, and called the natives to hear their stories about that picturesque locality. I will not say I was surprised—for one is never surprised about anything that happens in legendary history—but it did seem incongruous that the mountain, which had so impressed me with its beauty, should be associated, in aboriginal lore, with the most fearsome of all their mythical beings, the Ninya or Ice-men. In appearance those ancestral beings differ but little from the living aborigines, except that, because of their extreme coldness, their bodies are perpetually white with hoar-frost, and their beards and eyebrows masses of tinkling icicles.

Although Mt. Conner was their camp in *tjukurita* (creation) times, they now live under two salt lakes, about fifteen miles north. The entrance to their present abode, which is on a low island covered with stunted mulga, leads to huge underground caverns, whose ice-covered walls are continuously swept by howling, wintry blasts; a frightful place, equalled only in mythical history by the dreaded Nifelheim of the ancient Nordic people.

The Ninya-men spend their summer months in that glacial atmosphere; but when the winter nights come they leave their icy home to make long journeys over the rocky ranges and the sand-hills. The piercing winds that accompany them are responsible for the cold of winter, while the ice and frost that fall from their chilly bodies not only freeze the water-holes, but lodge in the grass to cut the feet of the natives; for it is one of the aboriginal beliefs that the deep cracks that form across the soles of their feet, and cause so much suffering in the winter mornings, are made by the ice left behind in the grass by the Ninya-men.

In spite of the fact that the Ninya can only be seen by the medicine men, the aborigines know, by an early morning mirage, when they are about. That sight, which only happens after still, cold, clear nights, seems to be confined to the desert areas. It is well known that the mirage of the hot, still days is the result of reflections from the surface of a layer of heated air, the refractive index of which is different from that of the atmosphere above it. In Central Australia, the conditions of the morning mirage are reversed. On the frosty mornings, the layer of still, cold air that lies close to the ground forms a reflecting surface from which

(a) "I saw many homes of the curious mulga-cnt . . . ." *(Page 58.)*
(b) "There is a spider . . . which coats each load of earth brought to the surface with a light silken web." *(Page 57.)*

". . . Matinya the new helper . . . revived our sinking spirits . . . ." (Page 62.)

hills can be seen in mid-air, trees reversed or dissociated from the earth, and the other distortions of a mirage. When a morning mirage does appear, the men assemble round their camp-fire, and chant a song which has the power, first, of 'putting the trees back in place,' then of hunting the Ninya-men to their underground home. Once that is achieved, the aborigines assert, the day becomes 'warm quick-fella.'

But those unpleasant Ice-men (there are no Ice-women) have their uses. When the hot winds of summer sweep across the country, killing the birds and the animals, and making life unbearable for the aborigines, the women and girls assemble at the clay-pan, near Anneri soak, to perform a ceremony that has the power of coaxing the Ninya from their icy caverns. The mere presence of their frigid bodies above the ground so reduces the air temperature that a cool breeze is created immediately.

Another legend associated with Anneri soak described a quarrel between two Ninya-men. Far back in *tjukurita* times the two men established a camp south of Mt. Conner, and lived by catching *mala* (*Lagorchestes hirsutus*), a small wallaby-like marsupial. For a while both men suffered from thirst, for neither could find a water-hole. One day, how-ever, the elder Ninya stumbled by chance on Anneri soak. Being, like all Ninya-men, selfish and greedy, he secretly quenched his thirst, covered the precious water-hole with boughs, and kept the news of his good fortune to himself. The younger Ninya became so thirsty that he was forced to open a vein in his leg, and drink his own blood to keep alive. The elder man, to deceive his companion, also smeared his leg with blood, but, of course, did not open the vein, for the water-hole had supplied his needs.

One day, as the younger man was hunting, he threw a stick, which just missed an escaping *mala* and fell, by pure chance, in Anneri soak. When the hunter saw the pool of water he became excited, and drank so greedily that the loud sucking noises attracted the attention of the older man, who ordered the thirsty hunter to leave the water alone. The famished man, however, continued to drink, even

F

though while so doing his companion beat him over the head. But as soon as his thirst was quenched he savagely returned the attack. They fought the whole day, dragging one another along the ground (causing the depression around the soak), and belabouring each other so badly that before the day ended both were dead. The icy blood that poured from the wounds of the Ninya-men is now large, white—not red—patches on the clay-pan floor, and their bodies two heaps of light-coloured quartzite on the summit of Mt. Conner.

Although the Ninya-men are the most important, there are several other 'Dream Time' ancestors associated with Mt. Conner. A little lizard, Tatiya, created some of the outlying hills, when searching for his boomerang, which had disappeared after glancing from the end of the mount; and a *wonambi* (gigantic mythical serpent) still lives in deep underground caves beneath a small spring on the mountain-side. The aborigines are so afraid of the *wonambi* that they will not go for a drink until one of their number makes a fire of blazing spinifex near the spring to scare the dangerous creature into its underground home.

Enquiries about the legends associated with Mt. Conner brought to light the fact that we had passed, on our outward journey, a number of sacred places that belonged to Tjikaba, the Ernabella man who was with us.

As we knew little about the mythology of those ranges, I was anxious to keep him in our party, so that on the homeward trip we could visit those localities and learn their sacred stories. Yet, although Tjikaba had been content to travel with us to Mt. Conner, he refused point-blank to go further, even though I offered him a liberal supply of flour, sugar and tobacco, his excuse being that he wanted to go 'pupping' (catching dingo pups, whose scalps are each worth a 50-lb. bag of flour).

'But,' I protested, 'if you will come with me I'll give you more flour than you can possibly earn by digging out dingo pups in the sand-hills, and besides, it won't be such hard work.'

'No you can't,' replied the aboriginal, in his native tongue, 'I can catch so many dingo pups at this time of the year, that your camels couldn't carry enough flour to pay for them.'

To prove his point he started to draw strokes in the sand, each one representing a dingo pup. When he had completed one row he began another, and even when that was finished he was not quite satisfied, so he added a few more, just to make sure.

He then sat back on his heels, looked at me, and asked:

'Have you enough flour to pay for that big mob of scalps?'

I admitted that it was beyond my resources, for it was evident that there was some reason, other than payment, behind his refusal.

'Why don't you want to come to Uluru (Ayers Rock) with me?' I asked bluntly.

'Because,' he explained, 'I'm afraid. The *mamus* at Ayers Rock kill all strangers, and you know that it's not my country.'

'But,' I said, 'I won't let the *mamus* hurt you. I'm a "big government man," and that'll frighten them.'

He agreed that I might be a 'very big' white man, but I could not stop a *mamu* from hurting a blackfellow, for the simple reason that I could not see them; which was correct enough, for only the medicine men have that power.

So I tried another angle. Would he wait for me at Anneri soak, and show me his *inma* (sacred places) on the way back to Ernabella? To that he readily agreed, and made arrangements to meet me at the soak when the moon was at the zenith at sunrise, and for us to light smokes as we travelled from Ayers Rock.

The three monoliths, Ayers Rock, Mt. Conner and Mt. Olga, are the most imposing and remarkable sights in Central Australia, and, of their kind, in the whole continent. They lie in an almost direct east-west line, and are so unlike in shape and structure that their origin constitutes one of the geological puzzles of that vast plain.

Mt. Conner is a flat-topped mass of quartzite, about two miles long and up to three-quarters of a mile wide, that towers about eight hundred feet above the plain. The base is a steep, talus slope, covered with huge boulders, from which rises a vertical rocky face, some three hundred feet high, that surrounds the mount almost without a break.

Although Mt. Conner is unscaleable for the most of its circumference, we were able to climb a broken section in the precipitous face on the south-western corner. The summit had a rocky, undulating surface, which was covered, at the time of our visit, with a surprisingly limited flora, consisting of no more than one species each of corkwood, eucalypt and spinifex. From the summit we had an extensive view of the surrounding country. The purple Musgrave Ranges to the south, contrasted strongly with the featureless mulga plains that extended to the misty eastern horizon. North of us were the salt lakes under which the Ninya-men lived, their surfaces shining like burnished metal in the late sunlight, whilst toward the west, sixty miles distant, the mysterious monolith of Ayers Rock rose out of the sandy desert, with Mt. Olga twenty miles beyond, so much in line that from where I stood it was not possible to separate the one from the other.

We returned to camp by a different route that involved the descent of a steep cliff. By then, my pavement-trained muscles and feet were getting tired, and inclined to give way in the steep, rough places. Ordinarily that would have passed unnoticed, but Matinya had recognized the signs and, without a word, watched over and guided my quaking footsteps. He was never more than a few paces from me, pushing dangerous boulders out of the way, breaking down bushes that obstructed the path, and suggesting, by signs, the best places for my feet. At one time some rolling stones caused me to lose my balance, and to fall backward, into the prickly centre of a spinifex bush, with the consequent explosive burst of language, proper to such occasions. Naturally I expected Matinya to laugh at the ludicrous sight of a white man sitting in a spinifex bush, but he quietly turned his

THE LEGEND OF THE LIZARD, TATIYA
". . . he frantically dug holes everywhere, until at last . . . he died." *(Page 82.)*

THE LEGEND OF THE MARSUPIAL MOLES
"Their wet weather shelter was a cylindrical cave at ground level." *(Page 82.)*

back, made no sign that he had seen the incident, and waited until I had extracted as many prickles as possible and was ready to continue the descent.

Toward sunset Tjundaga and I went to Anneri soak to give the camels their last drink before setting out on the journey to Ayers Rock. We found that the soak, after having been cleaned out, was far too deep for the camels to reach in safety. So we adopted the plan of covering a shallow trench with a tarpaulin, and pouring the water into it. From there the camels took their fill, the young ones boisterously, as do all young things, the older ones with dignity that belongs only to camels, while Dinimi, the oldest in the string, so old indeed that she could do little more than carry her saddle and an occasional child passenger, sat down sedately.

I did not return to the camp with the rest of the party, but sat by myself on the slope of a sand-dune, watching the grey shadows creep up the red mountainside, and the delicate colours of the twilight arc rise behind it.

CHAPTER X

The Journey to Ayers Rock

EVEN THOUGH MOANYA AND Matinya had been called to bring in the camels at the first grey light of dawn, and everything had been arranged for an early start, it was a good two hours after sunrise before we moved off.

It seemed almost impossible to get the camel string away earlier. Tjundaga and Nibiana were both easy-going folk who had meandered their way through life, so that a day or two, much less an hour or two, meant nothing to them. We knew that they were trying to get away as soon as possible, and that, in their minds at least, to leave an old camp by nine-thirty on a cold winter's morning was something of an achievement. We did not hurry them, nor, in fact, did we go near the loading except to attend our own camels, for had we shown any signs of impatience we should have confused everybody, and no time would have been gained.

As we were passing over the clay-pan, near Anneri soak, I could not help contrasting the appearance of Mt. Conner with how it had looked on the previous evening. Then it had been a blushing red; in the morning it was dark and forbidding, veiled in purple shadow. Remote, the mountain towered above the plain, like a walled and ancient castle on the crest of a rocky hill. The dust from the feet of the camels, rising in a soft, luminous haze, added still further to the illusion.

It was a strange sight. In the foreground was the string of twelve camels, their attenuated shadows stretching across the plain, led by the native men, and followed by the women, wooden dishes balanced delicately on their heads, fire-sticks smoking; while behind them all, like a back-drop, was the purple battlemented hill.

Just after leaving the soak we again passed through a large number of bushes of the dreaded camel poison

(*Duboisia hopwoodii*). This shrub had previously caused us an anxious time at Mt. Conner, for it is so poisonous that, should a camel so much as snatch a mouthful, he dies. But camels, such as Tjundaga's, which have lived in 'poison-bush' country for any length of time seem to learn that the plant is dangerous, and leave it alone. Nevertheless, I was anxious about the camels until several days had passed without mishap. Some camel-men assert that there is no antidote for the poison, while others say that liberal doses of Condy's crystals in water will save the beasts. Luckily we were not called upon to prove or disprove either of those assertions. It is a curious fact that, although *Duboisia hopwoodii* contains one of the most poisonous of the alkaloids, the aborigines on the eastern side of Australia chew the *Duboisia* after they have mixed the leaves with wood-ash, and discard the indigenous tobaccos. On the other hand, the natives who live in the desert regions of Central Australia chew the tobaccos, and use the *Duboisia* only for poisoning emus.

The journey from Mt. Conner to Ayers Rock led us across sixty miles of arid, trackless desert of sand-dunes. These dunes, which are about a third of a mile apart and from twenty to fifty feet in height, stretch across the country in parallel series for sometimes hundreds of miles. As our route was due west, and the trend of the sand-hills approximately north-east/south-west, we had to cross most of the ridges at right angles.

The task of negotiating a camel-string across those sand-hills, without breaking their nose-lines, called for both skill and patience. In fact, the total mileage that we could travel in a day depended almost entirely on the skill of the camel-men. Unnecessary hurry always meant the breaking of nose-lines, and the consequent loss of time in replacing them, for the camel had to be caught, a new cord made and fitted, and the beast tied back in the string. Never was the proverb 'More haste, less speed' so applicable as when travelling by camel across the sandy desert of Central Australia.

Although, in general, the string kept on its steady way,
there were always delays. Tjundaga and Nibiana were
aboriginal in both thought and outlook, and their hunting
instincts so strong that the mere sight of a fresh kangaroo
or wild turkey track, a goanna hole, or a honey ant's nest
was sufficient to turn the string from its rightful course, or
stop it altogether. Nibiana, from her lofty perch on the
seat of the camel, would then direct the investigation of the
track, or the digging-out of the nest. As time was limited,
I, unfortunately, could not allow these little excursions; if I
had there would have been far more hunting than travelling.
So, to prevent both delay and friction, I adopted the ruse,
as soon as the string stopped, of walking up to Nibiana and
enquiring casually, 'What's the matter?'

'Nodin',' Nibiana would say, with a guilty look on her
face, as she started the camels, 'me only little bit hungry
longa tummy for blackfella tucker.'

Though we could do nothing about the matter, Lauri and
I understood her desire for dainties. Camp fare, when it has
to be prepared at the end of a long day of travel, becomes
very monotonous.

As there was no track between Mt. Conner and Ayers
Rock, and as Tjundaga was a stranger to those parts, I had
taken a compass bearing on the Rock when we were at the
summit of Mt. Conner. On second thoughts I decided to
leave the route entirely to the camel-man, for I wanted to
know how accurately Tjundaga could retain his sense of
direction, and the means he would employ to reach Ayers
Rock without mechanical aids. The conditions were excellent
for these tests, for the moment we entered the sand-hill
country, Mt. Conner would be out of sight except from the
top of the higher dunes, and Ayers Rock invisible for the
first two days. No doubt Tjundaga had memorized the
direction, but it was not until the afternoon of the first day
that I noticed how simple, yet how efficient, was his method
of keeping on a straight course. It amounted to no more
than the lighting of thickets of spinifex as he passed along,
so that, when he reached the crest of a sand-ridge from
were he could look back to Mt. Conner, the line of 'smokes'

showed the course he had taken. Indeed, so accurate were Tjundaga's methods and sense of direction that, on the evening of the second day, when I climbed to the crest of an adjacent sand-hill, Ayers Rock, the sand-hill on which I stood, and Mt. Conner were in a straight line.

The following morning, when the camels were being loaded, I again climbed the sand-hill to renew my acquaintance with the Rock. I had been there some years previously, but for all too short a time, as my diary reveals:

We left at midday, with the camel-string leading us back to humdrum civilization and monotony. I followed on unwilling feet, for the lure of the great rock was upon me, calling me back to wander round its base, to look up at its mighty walls, to explore its numberless caves, and to hear the strange creation legends from its aboriginal owners.

Ayers Rock ranks among the wonders of Australia, if not of the world. It is an enormous monolith of metamorphosed granite. Its sides rise so abruptly that a person, standing on level ground, can rest his hands on precipices a thousand feet high.

Gosse, who discovered the Rock in 1873, wrote:

This rock is certainly the most wonderful natural feature I have ever seen.

Other travellers have told of its imposing beauty, its colouring and immensity, but, although they have spoken truly, it would be well nigh impossible to convey, by the written word, any sense of its grandeur and majesty. We travelled all day with the Rock growing larger and larger; in fact, after our lunch camp, it seemed as if every sand-hill must be the last. But it was nearing sunset before the camel-string reached the open plain which surrounds Ayers Rock, a plain swept clear by the local storms created by the monolith itself.

Although Lauri and I had walked ahead, it was long after sunset before we arrived at my old camp site, a few yards from the southern face of the Rock.

It was an eerie place. A perpendicular cliff, towering a thousand feet above us, shut out whatever light remained in the western sky. And in the gloom we could make out little but the ghostly forms of the trees, the dim shapes of the tumbled boulders and the ragged sky-line above. Lauri soon had a roaring fire going, for the night was cold, and the blazing logs seemed more companionable than the darkness. But the firelight intensified rather than lessened the strangeness, for whereas beforehand we could distinguish some of the details around us, the light entirely blotted them out, reducing our world to its own limited circle, an infinitesimal area in that mighty country.

We were listening to the approaching camel-bells, when I suddenly realized that, as Tjundaga did not know the country, he would think that our fire was a signal for direction, and make straight for it. As such a course would have led him into many deep gutters, I hastily took a lighted stick, and ran a line of fires from our camp to a position in the open plain where the ground was level. Tjundaga understood my signals, and in less than five minutes the silence was broken by the camels, the chattering of the natives, and the general hustle of unloading.

Tjundaga sat his camels in the only clear space he could find, but as it was a distance from our fire we asked Matinya to bring some blazing logs across to provide light for unloading. I was standing with the children, for they were distinctly nervous in those weird surroundings, when we saw Matinya returning. He was a fearsome sight. His legs were dimly visible by the light of the burning log he carried in his right hand, and his body, which could not be seen, was replaced by the glowing ends of the sticks that looked remarkably like red eyes. There was a cry of panic from the children as they made a quick rush for shelter, for they had mistaken Matinya for a *mamu*, one of their night-dwelling spirits. But the call of Matinya, and the laugh of Lauri and myself, quickly reassured them, and changed their cries of fear to sounds of mirth.

We camped near Maggie Springs, or to give it its more beautiful aboriginal name, Kapi Mutiguluna, which is situated in a deep bay and surrounded on all sides but one by perpendicular cliffs of over a thousand feet. The native men had lit the grass to show the track to the water-hole, and the effect of the flickering fire-light on those steep rock walls was most spectacular. I took Lauri to have a look at the water-hole, and then to a nearby cave of rock paintings which I had found on my previous visit. Lauri returned to camp, but I stayed on to make a copy of some of the designs.

It was a strange experience, working alone in that cave so late at night. The lamp went out before I had finished my task, but I sat on in the darkness. I felt dissociated from all that was real, as if I were in the presence of those who, for unknown years, had frequented the place, painted the curious symbols on the walls, and performed their sacred rites on the ground beside me. Everything was so still, not a single sound. Outside the cave was brilliant moonlight, but a shaft that had penetrated the darkness, and lit the earthen floor a few feet from where I sat, seemed only to accentuate the gloom.

I stayed long in that cave, sitting in the dust of ages of occupation, cogitating on the life of the aborigines before the arrival of the white man, and his dreadful treatment of them, treatment which had been brought vividly to mind because, in a small rock crevice a few hundred feet above my head, an escaping aborigine had met a tragic and unwarranted death.

A number of natives, who had been taken by a police protector of aborigines to be tried for various offences, had escaped. The policeman and his tracker, in pursuit of them, reached Ayers Rock and, while giving their camels a drink, saw the footprints of one of the escaping men on the sandy edge of the water-hole. The policeman stayed with the camels and sent the armed tracker to search for the escapees. The tracker came on one of them sitting on the top of an outcropping boulder, fired and hit him. The unfortunate aboriginal, unarmed and twice wounded, tried to conceal himself in a crevice, a little larger than his own body, under one of the huge fallen boulders. There the native was shot by the policeman, who claimed that his own life was in danger.

I had often wondered why an aboriginal, expert in the knowledge of tracks, and of hiding all traces of his presence, should have left his footmarks at the very place where they were sure to be seen, and why, with all the multitude of caves and crevices in the base and sides of Ayers Rock, he should have shown himself on the top of a boulder against the sky-line. Nor did I solve the mystery until I met old Kinkiba, one of the relatives of the dead man, at Mt. Conner.

I had been questioning the aborigines about the legends of Ayers Rock, and the conversations about them had started a flow of reminiscences, among them being the killing of that young aboriginal.

The old man told us the story of how, after the natives escaped, the tracker, armed by the policeman, fired on the escaping men while they were having a meal of wild peaches. The young man was shot in the chest, but was able, with the assistance of his companions, to reach Ayers Rock.

'Yokununa him properly sick fella,' explained old Kinkiba. 'Him know that s'pose him try to run away, policeman bin catch him, and kill him dead-fella.'

'Yokununa bin tell other blackfella,' old Kinkiba continued, 'me close-up bin finish (dead). You fella hide in *bulba* (cave) and when policeman bin kill me, you go 'long to Katatjuta (Mt. Olga).'

It turned out as the wounded man had planned. He indicated his presence by footmarks at the water-hole, then showed himself on the boulder. The tracker shot the wounded aborigine, who made his way into that tiny cleft and there met his end.

The policeman did not search for the other aborigines, which was what Yokununa had anticipated, but buried the dead man, little knowing how great a hero he had robbed of life.

Kinkiba told me the details of the young man's death purely as an incident. He did not seem to attach much importance to it, except to say that 'Yokununa was a good, quiet fella.'

Upper design—" . . . in one of the caves we found a complete picture story of an emu hunt." *(Page 88.)*
Lower design—"The artist . . . not knowing how to draw the horse . . . painted a kangaroo . . . and put the man on top." *(Page 86.)*

"Surely what we saw that afternoon was unique . . . a naked, brown-skinned man, painting a primitive symbol." *(Page 88.)*

CHAPTER XI

Ayers Rock and Its Legends

WE SPENT THE NEXT WEEK in an intensive study of the natural features of Ayers Rock, learning what we could, from its aboriginal inhabitants, about the meaning of the cave paintings and the legends belonging to the Rock.

Early in our stay, we walked round the Rock to get a general idea of its shape; but when I tried to draw a rough map, I was unable to remember the numerous deep bays and jutting headlands. First I called Lauri, and then Tjundaga, to help me out of the difficulty, but although each started off confidently, they were soon as hopelessly confused as myself. Our failure convinced us that it was necessary to make a survey, before we could hope to draw a ground plan on which to plot the legendary places.

Lauri and I spent a long and strenuous day on that work, determining the angles with a prismatic compass, our only surveying instrument, and pacing the intermediate distances. By those means we were able to get sufficiently accurate data to make a suitable map.

I am not surprised that we failed in our first attempt to draw that plan. Everything is on such an enormous scale that all estimates regarding distances were faulty. For instance, we thought that the depth of the bay in which Mutigulana water-hole is situated would not be more than one hundred and fifty yards, yet the survey showed it to be over three hundred, which, even then, was little greater than the height of the precipices that towered on either side.

The final plan showed the Rock to be roughly kite-shaped, and approximately two miles across the major diameters. Its long, straight, northern face—the direction from which most travellers approach—has given rise to the belief that the Rock is narrow and somewhat oval in form; an understandable mistake, for only an experienced cartographer could visualize the ground plan, without the assistance of either a survey or an aerial photograph.

As a natural feature the Rock is incomparable. One might liken Mt. Conner to a walled, mediaeval city; or Mt. Olga to a ruined temple, or palace of a bygone Pharaoh. But there seems to be nothing to which Ayers Rock can be

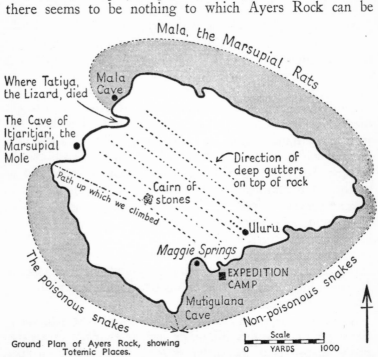

Ground Plan of Ayers Rock, showing Totemic Places.

likened. It is an enormous pebble, its sides so steep and so smooth that neither grass nor trees find a foothold, the only exception being an occasional fig-tree, whose long and twining roots somehow manage to hold on to the surface. To add still further to its singular appearance, the Rock is terra-cotta red, except at the head of some of the deep bays, where the surface has been stained black by the water-falls which pour over the precipices after the summer storms.

Because I lived so near the Rock—our camp was less than thirty yards from its vertical wall—I felt a greater liking for it than any other spot I have visited. Continually in the midst of work I found myself admiring the curves of the immense buttresses against the cloud-flecked sky, and the play of light and shade on the red sides; or at night, from the warmth of my sleeping-bag, tracing the contours of its velvet blackness against the glittering heavens.

When I saw Ayers Rock some years previously, I was almost over-awed by its size, its colour, its silence and its solitude, and in retrospect those were my only memories. But later, when I learned the legends of the place, of the Snakes which fought round Mutiguluna water-hole, of the Marsupial Rats and the evil Kulpunya, of the distraught Lizard and its lost boomerang, and of the harmless Marsupial Mole,[1] my outlook changed. The immense and beautiful surroundings were no longer mere precipices, caves or splashes of colour; they had been vitalized by the stories that the aborigines had told me; the precipices were the work of the little Lizard or the Marsupial Rats, the caves the one-time camping places of ancestral beings, and the grey smudge on the cliff the smoke-stain from the burning camp of the Sleepy Lizard-women.[2]

The major legend of Ayers Rock concerns a quarrel between the Windulka, Mulga Seed-men of Kikingura, on the western end of the Petermann Ranges, and the Kunia, Carpet Snakes and Mala, Marsupial Rats, of Ayers Rock.

At the time when the world was young, the Mulga Seedmen decided to initiate their youths, and, to make an occasion of it, asked the Bell-bird, Panpanpalana, to travel over the country and invite all the animals, birds and reptiles to attend.

So far as Ayers Rock is concerned, the story opens when the Bell-bird reached the home of the Carpet Snakes at Pukabuga, about eighty miles east of the Rock, and delivered the invitation. The Carpet Snakes, good-natured and peaceful in those days as now, accepted willingly and made ready for the journey. The Bell-bird then travelled to invite the Marsupial Rats which lived at Ayers Rock. But when he

[1] *Notoryctes typhlops.*　　　　[2] *Tiliqua scincoides.*

reached there, he found that they were in the midst of their own initiation ceremonies, and were not anxious to make the journey. He was able, however, to persuade them to accept.

The Carpet Snakes, on their way to Kikingura, spent the first night at the Uluru water-hole (now a deep catchment on the summit of Ayers Rock). While they were hunting on the following morning they met a number of Sleepy Lizard-women. The Carpet Snakes promptly forgot all about their promise to attend the ceremonies of the Mulga Seed-men, married the women and settled down at the Mutiguluna water-hole. The Marsupial Rats also put off the day of leaving, for their ceremonies were by no means finished.

Meanwhile the Mulga Seed-men waited, and when, after several days, there was still no sign of their guests, they sent the Bell-bird to find out the cause of the delay. The messenger returned to Ayers Rock and reminded the Carpet Snakes and the Marsupial Rats of their promises, but they both refused point-blank to keep them, the Snakes saying that they had just married and had no desire to travel, and the Marsupial Rats contending, somewhat rudely, that they were far too busy with their own ceremonies to be troubled about those of other people.

When the Bell-bird delivered the message, the Mulga Seed-men were so enraged over the discourtesy, that they asked their friends, the Poisonous Serpents, to destroy the Carpet Snakes, and instructed their own medicine men to prepare a punishment for the Marsupial Rats.

The Poisonous Serpents attacked the unsuspecting Carpet Snakes from two sides and quickly surrounded the camp. A mighty conflict followed, in which many were killed on both sides. The two leaders, Kunia Ungata, of the Carpet Snakes, and Kutitjilda, of the Serpents, fought each other with great courage and ferocity. Kutitjilda, severely wounded in the head, was retreating from the fray, when Tjintatjinta, the Willy Wagtail-woman,[1] attacked him savagely with her digging-stick and cut off his nose. One of the uninjured Serpents, Kulikudjeri, was so enraged over the defeat that,

---

[1] *Rhipidura leucophrys.*

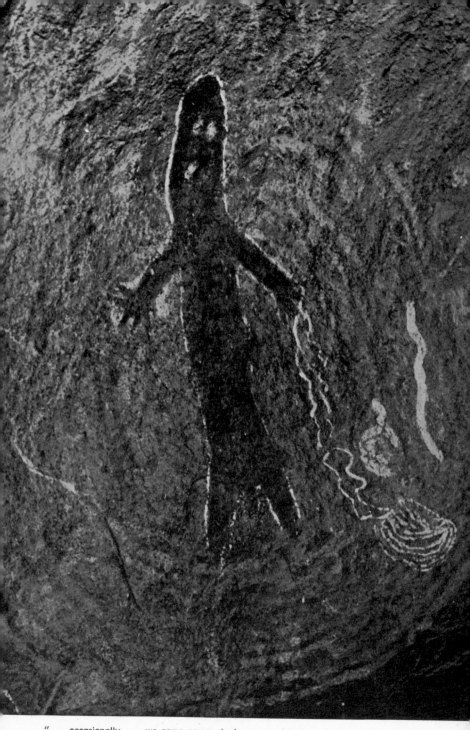

"... occasionally ... we came across single or group designs that were remarkably decorative and well-balanced." *(Page 89.)*

". . . and about ten miles distant, like a leviathan resting on the waterless billows of sand, was the great, red Rock . . . ." *(Page 93.)*

when he saw the harmless Sleepy Lizard-women, he burnt both them and their camp to cinders.

The Carpet Snakes that survived the struggle left their camp at the Mutiguluna water-hole and retreated eastward along the Rock, taking their wounded leader with them. But he died from his wounds, and his followers, overcome with grief, clustered round his dead body and killed themselves with a lethal chant.

While that battle was in progress, the medicine men of the Mulga Seed-people were busy making a malignant being, called Kulpunya, with which to punish the Marsupial Rats. After they had laid out the skeletal frame—a mulga branch for a backbone, forked sticks for ears, women's hair along the back, the teeth of a small marsupial at one end and the tail of a bandicoot at the other—the medicine men spent the rest of the day chanting songs of magic to fill their creation with the spirit of evil. Then, from sunset to sunrise, they left it alone, for it was only during the hours of darkness that such a creature could develop.

The following morning, the evil thing was already showing signs of life; hair was growing along its back, the teeth had increased in size, and the feet were sprouting. Again the medicine men sat round Kulpunya and chanted songs which were so effective that during the next night it actually crawled some distance. The creature was brought back to camp, and the final songs were chanted, to imbue it with hatred and malice toward all strangers.

On the day fixed for the attack, Kulpunya was fully developed. He was about the size of a dog, but had no hair on his body, except along the back and at the point of the tail. The transplanted teeth had grown to formidable dimensions, and his malevolence had greatly increased.

The Mulga Seed-men then ordered Kulpunya to go to Ayers Rock and destroy the Marsupial Rats. When Kulpunya reached his destination everyone was having an afternoon sleep, except Lorin, an old Kingfisher-woman, who had been expecting an attack from the Mulga Seed-men for some time. She had made her camp apart, so that she could

G

get a better view of the country. But her precautions were of little avail, for, although she saw Kulpunya coming and called out loudly, she was unable to wake the people before he had attacked and killed some of them. The rest of the people, terrified by the sudden assault, left Ayers Rock and fled in confusion to the south-west.

The legend of the Poisonous Serpents and the Carpet Snakes belongs almost entirely to the southern face of the Rock, and that of the Marsupial Rats and Kulpunya to the northern. Two other ancestors of minor importance, who seem to have been undisturbed by the troublesome Mulga Seed-men and their allies, lived at and created most of the western side. They were a group of Marsupial Moles, Itjatitjari, and a little Lizard, Tatiya.

The Moles interfered with no one, but spent most of their time searching for food. Their wet weather shelter is a cylindrical cave at ground level, and their summer, or dry weather camp, an enormous bowl-shaped depression high up the Rock.

The little Lizard, Tatiya, had originally lived on a salt lake not far from the original home of the Carpet Snakes. One day, whilst trying out a boomerang, he threw it so far westward that it struck Mt. Conner, and, glancing off, landed somewhere near Ayers Rock. The little Lizard was so distraught over his loss that, after searching round Mt. Conner without success, he ran as quickly as possible to Ayers Rock. But still he could not find the boomerang. Thinking that it had become buried in the sand, he frantically dug holes everywhere, until at last, from sheer worry, his bowels dropped out, and he died.

Before those mighty doings of 'Creation Times,' Ayers Rock, as the monolith of today, did not exist; but after the Snakes had fought their battles, the Marsupial Rats had been driven away by the fiendish Kulpunya, and the little Lizard and the harmless Moles had finished their work, the great Rock rose out of the ground, even as it is today.

Every precipice, cave, gutter and mark on the top and the sides of the Rock commemorate the exploits and adventures of the creatures of those long-distant times. The gutters, rock strata and weather stains on the southern face were the tracks of the warring Snakes; the northern precipices, with their numberless caves, were the camping places of the Marsupial Rats; and the innumerable pot-holes on the western side were the work of the little Lizard and the harmless Moles.

Chapter XII

We Climb the Rock

ULURU WATER, ON THE SUMMIT of Ayers Rock, where the Carpet Snakes made their first night camp, is an important spot in aboriginal mythology. The aborigines from the east, the west and the south had told me about the gigantic, many-coloured *wonambi* (mythical snake) which lives beneath its surface.

For years I had looked forward to visiting the water-hole, though I knew that to reach it meant a long, hazardous climb up the crest of a steep saddle on the south-western corner. But when I saw that bare, dangerous slope, leading upward into the sky, entirely devoid of grass or trees which would help in the ascent, my courage failed, and I persuaded myself that any information gained by a visit to Uluru would not be worth the risk and the labour involved.

However, the day that Moanya, Matinya and Tjundaga took me to the upper edge of the dry-weather camp of the Marsupial Mole, I realized that we were about a third of the way to the summit, and had already climbed some of the steepest grades. So I decided to make the complete ascent and get the matter of Uluru over, once and for all. I told the aborigines of my decision, and sent Tjundaga down with a message to Lauri, so that his mind would be at rest over my long absence. But when we started, the aborigines, instead of going back on our tracks until we reached the main crest, which is the best way to the summit, climbed straight up the side of the saddle.

But they soon found out their mistake, for within a few yards the angle became so acute that we were forced to lie on our sides, and use the combined effort of hands and feet to pull ourselves up a few inches at a time. It was an arduous task; a yard or so of climbing, a rest to regain our breath, a few more yards, another rest, and so on until the danger point was passed. My native companions were most solicitous for my safety, warning me about the loose fragments of the surface, and pointing out the best places to put my feet.

Once we reached the crest of the saddle, which, although steep, was wide and fairly smooth, there was much less danger of an accident, so long as we did not trip, tread on one of the many thousands of detached fragments of the surface, or, most important of all, lose our nerves.

On the highest point of the Rock some previous visitor had built a low cairn of stones around a glass screw-topped bottle, in which were the names of people, who in recent years had climbed Ayers Rock, and, I am afraid, many who had not.

Although Gosse, the discoverer, made the ascent in 1873, the earliest record was that of W. McKinnon, who noted that he had taken away a match-box left behind by Alan Breadon of Henbury Station many years previously. There were also the names of some members of the McKay party, *all* the members of the Foy party, and of others who sought, but did not expect to find, the fictitious Lasseter's reef. I added my name to that illustrious throng.

From the cairn I could look down on our camp. At first I could not pick out the tents, and when I did they looked so small that it was difficult to realize they were eight feet square; they seemed rather like small fragments of quartz lying amid the spinifex.

The top of the Rock is remarkable. I had expected to see trees, shrubs and grasses, but, except for a few low bushes, an odd bunch or so of spinifex, and a much battered cork-wood tree near the cairn, there was nothing to clothe its bare surface. The summit is scored with deep gutters that lie south-east/north-east, and which, Matinya explained, were the tracks of the Carpet Snakes as they travelled from Pukabuga to Uluru in 'Creation Times.' In actual fact the gutters are caused by the differential weathering of the vertical rock strata.

To reach the northern side, where Uluru water is situated, we had to walk across those gutters at right angles. Many of them were from ten to twenty feet deep, with sides so vertical that it was often difficult to find a place to cross. To my surprise I was able, in my rubber shoes, to climb slopes impossible to the aborigines, as the hardened soles of their feet slipped on the smooth surface.

But our effort was in vain. Although Matinya had not been to the top of Ayers Rock before, he felt quite sure, from the description the old men had given him, that he could find Uluru. But when he saw the hundreds, if not thousands, of circular pot-holes which had weathered out in the trough-like gutters, he became confused, and, after much searching, had to admit that he was beaten.

We reached ground level in the middle of the afternoon and, after eating a meal which Lauri had prepared, visited one of the curious cylindrical caves, associated with the initiation ceremonies of the Marsupial Rats, in which I had seen some paintings on my previous visit. Extending along the back wall, up to about the height of one's elbow, was a dark brown band of human blood which had been poured out from the arms of the men during the secret rituals, and above that band were the primitive paintings of the Pitjendadjara tribesmen.

There is little doubt that the paintings of the Pitjendadjara tribe, of which Ayers Rock is a veritable storehouse, are among the most primitive examples of the art of living people. But, in spite of their primitive nature, the art is by no means a dead expression, continuously repeating old formulae and taking nothing from the world about it, for alongside of, and in some places actually obscuring, faded ceremonial designs are present-day paintings of white men shooting bullocks, and, at one place, a man on horse-back. The artist, desiring to picture something he had seen, but not knowing how to draw a horse, did the next best thing. He painted a kangaroo, with its legs pointing toward the ground, and put the man on top. It was easy to detect the long ears, the thick, tapering tail and the short front legs of the marsupial.

It is certain that few, if any, of the paintings in that cave, or in the extensive series in the Mutiguluna rock shelter, were of any great age, for rain and exposure to the elements would have faded the designs. A series of photographs, taken at five-year intervals, showed that many of the designs recognizable in 1930 were faint, and some examples not decipherable ten years later.

A few days previously, when Lauri and I were copying the designs in another cave, we had asked both Moanya and Matinya to make a painting on the cave wall, just to show us how it was done, but they demurred on the ground that it would use too much red ochre. I did not press the matter, for red ochre is possibly the most expensive material in their culture. When we were at Mt. Conner, Moanya had given an aborigine a spear for a block of red ochre about the size of his fist, and it would have taken him two days of almost continuous work to make that spear. Red ochre is, in fact, the cosmetic of the aborigines. Both men and women delight in rubbing it over their bodies, for it not only rids the skin of its accumulated dust, but gives to it that attractive bronze-like appearance so desired by all aborigines.

But on the day when we were in the cave of the Marsupial Rats I had some red ochre with me (I had traded a red handkerchief with Nibiana for it), so we were able to see for the first time the complete technique of a cave painting. It could hardly have been simpler. Moanya, with the addition of water, ground the two pigments, red ochre and white pipe-clay, into a smooth paste on the surface of flat stones. Then, with his forefinger, he painted on the cave wall a design in red, representing a Fig Tree-ancestor from Jirinjirin, a place in the Musgrave Ranges. When the fundamental design was completed, the artist, stripping some bark from a nearby tree, and using it as a brush, outlined the figure in white pipe-clay.

The finished painting showed a male figure, in which the conventional head was replaced by a wide circle with radiating lines projecting from the upper edge. This circle, the artist explained, was the *nuiti* (head-dress) worn by the

Fig Tree-men in 'Creation Times.' Moanya looked at me in surprise when I asked him where was the face, the nose, the eyes and the mouth, and said that there was only one place where they could be, in the middle of the *nuiti*, which, as I ought to know, entirely surrounds the face. He explained that he did not trouble to draw the face, because every blackfellow would know where it was. Though I was a white man, he did not expect that I would ask such a foolish question.

Surely what we saw that afternoon was unique; there a naked, brown-skinned man painted a primitive symbol, which was comparable in both design and technique with those produced by our forefathers of the Old Stone Age in Europe, twenty thousand years ago. It seemed as if the hands of time had been turned back through all those many centuries.

There are two schools of thought on the function of primitive art. One contends that the urge to draw is a propensity of the human mind, and that all true art is a spontaneous activity carried out for its own sake. The other school takes the opposite view and claims that the primitive man is essentially practical, and would not waste his time making pictures, say of animals, just for amusement, but rather that he draws animals to gain a magical control over them, so that they can be more easily captured in the hunt.

There is no doubt that in some parts of Australia certain paintings are believed to possess magical power over the elements; and others, maybe, over the animals, although about the latter the evidence is not so complete. But it is extremely doubtful whether the paintings at Ayers Rock were done for this reason. For instance, in one of the caves we found a complete picture-story of an emu hunt: the emu, the tracks of the hunters, the marks of the wounded bird and the dragging spear, and the place where the bird was finally caught, killed and eaten. Everything that was necessary to catch and kill that bird by sympathetic magic was in that painting. Yet, when I asked Matinya and the other men the significance of the painting, they claimed that it was nothing more than the record of a successful hunt, and was in no way related to the capturing of emus. They further explained that when hunting emus they use magical chants and other rites to make the birds stupid, so that they could be approached more easily. Later, when in the Mann Ranges, we saw a rock-marking that commemorated the occasion when Moanya himself had run down an emu on a hot day. That certainly was something to commemorate!

The paintings in the caves at Ayers Rock are the work of many different hands, done at many different times. They show no sense of unity; in fact, in the Mutiguluna cave there is so much over-painting that we sometimes found it difficult to separate one design from another. Yet, occasionally, in some remote cave or sheltered rock-face, we came across single or grouped symbolic designs that were of remarkable design and good balance. Although those designs are not works of art of high merit, they do show that there are many individuals in primitive societies who possess that sense of balance, rhythm and proportion which must be inherent in every true artist.

When at dusk we arrived home, stiff and sore, but pleased with the day's work, we found the camp in an uproar. Just before sunset one of the children had come back with the news that, whilst playing in a cave near the camp, he had seen splashes of fresh blood on the rocky floor. Everyone was convinced that it was the mark of a *kadaitcha*. The *kadaitcha*, according to aboriginal belief, is a man, practically invisible, armed with a knowledge of special chants, who has been sent out to avenge the infringement of some important tribal law. When he nears the wanted person, he cuts his body, and allows the blood to flow on the rock surface.

At the time, my mind was so full of the legends and the day's research that I did not attach much importance to the rumour. It was only when, after tea, I went across to ask Tjundaga and Matinya if they would interpret some drawings, that I realized what a thorough fright everyone had received. All of them, even Tjundaga and Nibiana, were so fearful of attracting the attention of the dreaded *kadaitcha*

man, that the fires they crouched round were so small they
could barely be seen. Nibiana would not even come to do
our washing-up until I lent her a torch, and when she did
arrive she had Tjundaga's shot-gun under her arm.

The whole of the native folk undoubtedly had the jitters.
Moanya was particularly afraid. He thought that he had
been specially singled out on account of the painting he had
made, without the owner's permission, in the sacred cave
of the Marsupial Rats. He prevailed upon Lauri to lend
him a rifle with which to scare away the *kadaitcha* man,
should he appear when the camels were being brought in the
following morning. Moanya said that he did not want any
cartridges, only the rifle.

'Him strong fella, *kadaitcha*,' said the frightened aboriginal, his large dark eyes flashing. 'S'pose him bin see us,
we all bin dead fella in the mornin'.'

Before the evening was over all the men, women and
children came across to our camp, for our fire was large and
warm, and besides, they assured us, it was much safer there,
for we had many 'cleva' things, and so no *kadaitcha* man
would dare to come near the place.

When we had finished our evening's work the aborigines
went back to their camps, but they must have spent a most
uncomfortable night, for a bitterly cold wind raged round
the Rock, and they were afraid to stoke their fires lest they
exposed themselves to the unseen danger.

Lauri and I had no doubt that the whole incident was the
result of a panic, but no one could be quite certain what
effect such a fright would have on a people with so strong
a belief in the *kadaitcha* man and his kind. It would have
been a simple matter for one of the natives to get the idea
that he had been 'boned' or magically attacked; if that had
happened, we should have had little chance of saving his
life, unless we could have quickly secured the help of one of
their medicine men. So I was much relieved next morning
when Tjundaga informed me that the *kadaitcha* had not
attacked anyone during the night, and that no one was any
the worse for the fright.

After breakfast Lauri and I assembled all who had any knowledge of the affair, and suggested that we should go along to have a look at the blood left behind by the *kadaitcha*. So, with the youngsters, Matinya, who also claimed to have seen the blood, and Tjundaga—with his rifle—we climbed the steep slope to inspect the tell-tale marks. But none could be found, although the children were certain that the splashes of blood had been there on the previous evening. I then insisted that Matinya should show me those he had seen, but after much searching a crest-fallen Matinya had to admit they had disappeared, although he still claimed that on the previous evening he had distinctly seen *four* drops.

Then every man assured every other man he knew that the youngsters had made a mistake—they did not say anything about Matinya—and that they, personally, were not afraid. Tjundaga told me several times on our way back to camp that 'They (the aborigines) couldn't put the wind up him.' But we were careful not to ask him why, on the previous evening, his camp-fire was as small as that of any other native, or why, at that moment, he was carrying a rifle.

CHAPTER XIII

Our Visit to Katatjuta

OUR NEXT STOPPING PLACE, Mt. Olga,[1] or in the aboriginal tongue, Katatjuta (heads, many), has been well named by its native owners.

We were anxious about the Walpanya rock-hole, situated at the foot of Mt. Olga, because 'Snowy' Pearce had warned us that it had failed on several occasions during recent years. So I asked Matinya about it.

'Him *kapi-bulka* (water, large),' replied Matinya, enthusiastically.

Now I had been caught by these *kapi-bulka* water-holes before. The aborigines, requiring only enough water for a drink, look on a catchment of perhaps twenty gallons as large, whereas twenty times that amount would be insufficient for our party, particularly if the camels were thirsty. So I again questioned Matinya to try to get some idea of its relative size.

'Is Walpanya as big as Anneri at Atila (Mt. Conner)?' I asked.

'Yes,' replied the native brightly, 'Walpanya him big water, more bigger than Anneri.'

'What about Mutiguluna (at Ayers Rock),' I went on. 'Bigger than that?'

'Him big fella water,' asserted Matinya. 'More bigger than Mutiguluna. Him as big,' and then the native paused, 'him as big, as big as the sea belonga white man.'

I gave up, for obviously Matinya had pushed his imagination to the limit. Mutiguluna is one of the largest and most reliable waters in the whole of the western desert, and Matinya had never seen the ocean.

After that information, or lack of it, I told Tjundaga that it would be necessary to complete the journey to Walpanya

1 To prevent confusion, when describing the legendary stories, Katatjuta will refer to the whole group, and Mt. Olga, named by Giles in 1872, to the highest point.

in one day, and that we would have to leave early, as it was over twenty miles distant. But in spite of my instructions, it was well after ten o'clock before the last package was aboard, and we moved off.

Looking back from our lunch camp, I was surprised at the difference between the appearance of Ayers Rock from the eastern and western sides. Viewed from the east, the outline of the Rock was made up of smooth, rounded curves, which were scored from top to bottom with vertical strata; from the west, it had a comparatively flat top, and almost perpendicular sides, marked with thousands of circular pot-holes of varying dimensions.

We had camped for lunch at one of the best positions from which to see Ayers Rock. Nearby were the terra-cotta sand-hills, dotted with the grey of the solanums and the eremophilas. Stretching out before us was a wide, sandy flat, covered so thickly with spinifex in seed that it resembled a wheat field ready for harvest. Spotted on the flaxen-yellow plain were the graceful, dark-foliaged desert-oaks (*Casuarina decaisneana*), and, about ten miles distant, like a leviathan resting on the waterless billows of sand, was the great red Rock, with the purple cloud-shadows drifting slowly across it.

By the middle of the afternoon, it was evident that we were not going to reach the water-hole before dark, and I think Tjundaga and Nibiana had an idea that I would not be insistent about the matter. But when, in the late afternoon, they stopped the string and started to make a fire, I quickly upset such ideas by telling them that, right or wrong, I was going to camp at the Walpanya rock-hole that evening, not in the middle of the desert. Nibiana gave vent to a burst of language most unbecoming to a lady, mounted her camel, and started the string on its way again. Nevertheless, I did not feel a hard task-master, for we had made a late start, and both Lauri and I were anxious about the water-hole.

It was half-past seven before we stopped on the western side of Katatjuta, near two huge pillars between which the

Walpanya rock-hole is situated. This water takes its name from the gorge Walpanya (walpa—wind), so called because, the aborigines told us, there is always a strong wind blowing in it, even on the stillest of days.

Lauri and I had just finished our meal when we saw Matinya quietly pick up a fire-stick and walk away, obviously to see if the water was up to expectations. We followed, lamp in hand.

I shall not forget that walk to Walpanya. Within a short distance from the mouth of the gorge, the high walls closed in quickly, and the gloom became so deep that we had a difficulty in making our way among the huge fallen boulders on the floor of the gorge. By the time we had reached the rock-hole, a walk of about four hundred yards, there was no light whatever. The lamp that we carried lit but a small circle, and all else was intense darkness. It was only when we looked upwards that anything could be seen, and there, laid out on a sparkling sky, was the great curve of Scorpio that seemed to rest on the tomb-like blackness of the chasm walls.

Matinya's rock-hole 'as big as the sea' was disappointingly small, about thirty gallons of green, stagnant water, only just enough, as we found out next morning, to provide a drink for two of the camels. I think that Matinya, like ourselves, was surprised at its smallness, although he carried off an awkward moment most successfully by waving his smoking fire-stick over the diminutive supply and saying, with a bright smile, 'Kapi pulya, kapi bulka' (water good, water large).

Some years later I found out that Matinya's original statement would have been more or less correct in a good season, for then not only are the extensive rock-holes filled, but a creek runs from the mouth of the gorge into the open plain.

Early next morning Tjundaga and I walked to the Walpanya rock-hole and found it was too thick and foul for drinking, except in an extremity. So we decided to make the water in our canteens last as long as possible, and then

return to Ayers Rock. As the weather was cool, we estimated
that we would have enough water to last our party for
about three days, without inflicting undue hardship. However, to safeguard ourselves, we moved to the eastern side
of Katatjuta, where, in an emergency, we would be within
about six hours of Ayers Rock.

Katatjuta is a most spectacular place. It consists of thirty
or more enormous round-topped pillars of a particularly
coarse conglomerate, the highest of them, Mt. Olga, tower-
ing fifteen hundred feet above the plain. Some of the pillars
are isolated, some stand close to their neighbours, but practically all of them are separated from the next by almost
perpendicular-sided chasms which extend almost to ground
level, and are often so narrow at the base that it is only just
possible to squeeze through.

Although many of the pillars of Katatjuta are higher than
Ayers Rock, and the scenery magnificent to a superlative
degree, the surroundings did not give me that feeling of
immensity which I experienced at Ayers Rock, but reminded
me rather of a primordial world, as though I had stepped
backward into some geological age, where wide-winged
pterodactyl soared around the high domes, and giant dino-
saurs lumbered their ungainly way along the bases.

When Ernest Giles visited the place in 1873 he apparently
gained a similar impression, for he wrote:

The appearance of Mt. Olga from this camp is truly wonderful;
it displayed to our astonished eyes rounded minarets, giant cupolas,
and monstrous domes. There they have stood as huge memorials
from the ancient times of earth, for ages, countless eons of ages, since
its creation first had birth. Time, the old, the dim magician, has
ineffectively laboured here, although all the powers of oceans at his
command; Mt. Olga remained as it was born.

The object of our visit was not only to record the legends,
but to link them with the outstanding natural features. We
found that three separate groups of aboriginal ancestors were
responsible for Katatjuta. The pillars of the south-western
corner, including Mt. Olga, are the metamorphosed bodies
of the Kangaroo, the Euro (a hill kangaroo) and the little

Night-Owl; the domes on the eastern side are the former dwelling places of the Mice-women; and the double row of isolated pillars, rising over a thousand feet, on the western side the camps of the Pungalunga-men.

The Kangaroo and Euro, whose legendary journeys extend over many hundreds of miles, seem to have been rather benign persons, living peacefully with each other, but quarrelling occasionally with the little Night-Owl on account of his incessant talking. The Mice-ancestors, a closely-knit community of women, did little else but travel the desert in search of food by day, and return to their camps by night, neither troubling nor being troubled by anyone. The Pungalunga-men, on the other hand, although human in form, were fierce, cannibalistic creatures, their heads tower-ing above the tallest tree, their steps so long that few birds could travel faster, and their arms so powerful that even the boulders with which they played were higher than a man.

In those distant times, the Pungalunga hunted human beings for food, and usually returned to their camp at night carrying a number of dead men tucked under their hair-string belts, in much the same way as the aborigines of today carry the dead marsupials. Old Tjalerina explained to us, with a certain amount of horror and considerable detail, how the Pungalunga-men prepared the human food for cooking, and the orgy that followed.

After the Poisonous Serpents had suffered their defeat at Ayers Rock, they went to Katatjuta and persuaded the Pungalunga to accompany them to the Tomkinson Ranges, so that they could wreak vengeance on the harmless Snakes of the Kunduna water. But the Snakes were so well pre-pared and powerful that they were able to destroy all the hateful crew.

Even after those great creatures had left, and their camps had changed into pillars of stone, a human Pungalunga had lived at Katatjuta. He was as large as his forebears, so large indeed that, when hunting wallabies—for there were not enough human beings to provide him with sufficient food—

". . . a remarkable spire of rock called Pupiana that overshadowed our camp." *(Page 99.)*

Matinya seated on the edge of Uluru rock-hole, watching for signs of the mythical snake. *(Page 103.)*

he could walk with ease from the top of one monolith to another, a mere two to three hundred yards. His end came when he tried to step across Walpanya gorge on a cloudy day, misjudged his distance, fell to the bottom and died. I asked Tjalerina if there were any remains, such as there would have been if the Pungalunga had belonged to the 'Creation' period; but he replied that the Pungalunga was human, not *tjukurita* (ancestral) and would have disintegrated in the weather like any other man.

When collecting legends, it is sometimes difficult to find out whether one's informants are speaking of the long-distant past or of present-day events. This merging of the past and the present has confused some investigators, and convinced them that the eating of human flesh is a normal practice among the aborigines.

Perhaps the worst offender in this respect is Mrs. Daisy Bates in *The Passing of the Aborigines*, for, misled by rumours and legendary tales, she makes many references to cannibalism in her book. However, an examination of those accounts show that they are all based on stories of what had happened in the past, or hearsay evidence of the doings of natives in distant places.

As several references in *The Passing of the Aborigines* had been made about cannibalistic practices of the aborigines of the Mann and Musgrave Ranges, the people with whom I was working, I asked them, when the Pungalunga-men were being discussed, if any of their tribe had ever eaten human flesh. They were horrified, and indignantly disclaimed any knowledge of such a custom among themselves; but, they added, the aborigines to the south, that live along the railway line, were man-eaters, and hunted the tribes to the north of them.

Tjalerina then told me how the victims were cooked and eaten, using methods, by the way, suspiciously like those of the Pungalunga-men. Old Tjalerina went on to say that the white woman who lived at Ooldea—he did not know her name—always attended those man-eating feasts, but he felt fairly sure she only looked on; she did not eat anything.

H

And so does rumour damn us! For it goes without saying that the stories of my companions, and without doubt those of Mrs. Bates, are quite untrue; just rumours that grew up out of the belief that it is always the distant folk, the foreigners, who do the cruel and terrible things, while our neighbours, whom we meet and know, are decent and kindly folk.

Unfortunately those reports of cannibalism, although unsupported by evidence gained from research, either before or since the publication of the book, have been given wide circulation, and thus created an entirely wrong impression about a simple and kindly people.

From the description of previous travellers, we had expected to find that Katatjuta, which is about four miles long and two wide, would be a mass of domes like those of the outer perimeter. But as our work progressed we were surprised to find that it was made up of an almost complete circle of lofty monoliths grouped round a comparatively level space.

From the centre, which I reached on the last day of our stay, the scenery was magnificent. It was an artist's paradise, which made me wish whole-heartedly for a day to spend on nothing else but pictorial photography. But time, and an almost exhausted water supply, prevented that indulgence, even though I did make a number of exposures of the surroundings, the desert trees, and the spinifex.

The spinifex clumps are always a beautiful sight towards the end of the day, for then the light transforms their long, flexible seed-stems into a myriad lines of luminous golden-yellow, which bend gracefully with every passing breeze. Yet in spite of that ephemeral beauty, a walk through spinifex is a mild form of torture, for its innumerable needle-pointed spines are so sharp that they pierce even thick socks and heavy clothing.

That I had good cause to learn, for I was specially interested in feet and easy places on which to put them. The sharp stones of Katatjuta had reduced my last pair of strong boots to ribbons, and I was forced to wear canvas shoes, with thin rubber soles, that offered little protection for my feet either against spinifex, jagged stones, or the uneven surfaces of the steep slopes.

Until I had walked in such shoes, where every slip and stumble meant pain, I had not noticed how the aborigines chose a good foothold for every step they took. No doubt their actions were unconscious, or at least automatic from long practice, for they picked suitable places without apparent effort, while the whole of my attention was fully occupied in searching for smooth and level surfaces.

By the morning of the fourth day we were preparing to leave, for there was less than a gallon of water in the canteens.

As I wanted to make a cine shot of a remarkable spire of rock called Pupiana that overshadowed our camp, and needed some movement in the foreground, I asked Tjundaga to lead his camel-string along the valley at its base. Meanwhile I took a short cut through the hills, so as to be in position when he arrived.

I set up the camera, then looked for the string, but it was nowhere to be seen. For a while I was not unduly troubled, for the short cut would have put me well ahead of Tjundaga; but, after waiting for half an hour in a strong, icy wind, I was vexed when I saw by the smoke signals that the camel-string was well on its way to Ayers Rock.

It turned out that Tjundaga, having gone hunting with Lauri, had forgotten to pass my instructions on to Nibiana, who had set out blithely on her way, totally oblivious to the fact that she had left more than half of the party behind.

As the absence of the camel-string made the first position unsuitable, I had to find another—no easy task on steep slopes covered with masses of broken boulders, dead trees and spinifex.

Meanwhile old Tjalerina was wandering about aimlessly with a blazing fire-stick in his hand, trying to keep himself warm. Just as I had found a new place, and the clouds and lighting on the subject were ideal, some embers, which had dropped from his fire-stick, lit a bunch of spinifex on the windward side of me. The flames, driven by a strong wind, came towards me with the speed of an express train, barely allowing time enough for me to carry the camera out of harm's way, before the fire swept over the place where I had stood.

I was more than annoyed, for surely that was the last straw, and relieved my feelings considerably by telling Tjalerina—in English—my candid and immediate opinion of him. The poor old man was most contrite. He had already tried to put out the fire, but had about as much chance of extinguishing that explosive blaze, in such a wind, as one would have of putting out a burning oil refinery with a water pistol.

Again I had to find another position, and was just about to take the much delayed photograph when I noticed the aborigines, whom I had placed in the foreground, were laughing. For a moment I was puzzled as to the cause of their merriment until, on turning round, I saw old Tjalerina, his face wreathed in smiles, telling his companions on the hillside, by gesture and hand-signs, about the incident of the burning spinifex, and my subsequent behaviour.

For a while the old man was so busy with his story that he did not notice I was watching, and, when he did so, the speed with which his fingers stopped their movement, and the smile left his face, was so ludicrous that I forgot my annoyance and, much to Tjalerina's relief, laughed with the rest.

Still, all's well that ends well—the picture, in spite of the vicissitudes of its birth, turned out to be a gem in glowing colour.

It was a good three miles' walk before we reached the camels, and set out for our destination. However, even with the bad start, we made good time and by sunset were unloading at our old camp beside Ayers Rock.

"I saw old Tjalerina telling his companions, by gesture and hand signs, about the incident of the burning spinifex." *(Page 100.)*

". . . an island of sunburnt rocks pushed its way through the grassy surface to provide a home for the native pines (Callitris sp.) . . . ." *(Page 110.)*

CHAPTER XIV

We Return to Ernabella

ON OUR PREVIOUS STAY AT Ayers Rock, Lauri, Matinya and Tjundaga had climbed to the summit and located Uluru the day after Matinya and I, though reaching the top, had been unable to find the water-hole. But though at the time I was disappointed at our failure, because of the importance of Uluru in aboriginal mythology, I did not attempt the second climb, for the unusual slope of the descent had strained a tendon in my knee and given me a good deal of pain. Fortunately, the trouble disappeared after a day or two, and as it did not return when I scaled the steep slopes of Katatjuta I decided to make another attempt to see Uluru.

Matinya and I set off on a miserably cold morning; the sky was clouded, and an icy wind raged round the base of the Rock. In spite of the blazing fire-stick which Matinya carried, we stopped several times to light a clump of spinifex so that Matinya could warm himself, for the poor fellow was almost frozen. Had I not been with him, the aboriginal would have lit a fire under one of the boulders and stayed there until the day became warm. Unfortunately for him he was with a white man, who, a slave of the inexorable calendar and clock, had to return to a certain place, on a certain day, at a certain time.

When we started to climb, Matinya fortified himself with yet another blazing fire-stick, as thick as his arm, to minimize the effect of the cold. The wind had been troublesome enough at ground level, but when we were approaching one of the most difficult grades, about a third of the way to the top, the gale was terrific. The impact of its blast, and the steep slope, made the ascent particularly arduous. We would struggle up until exhausted, then lie flat on the rock, like a pair of lizards, to gain sufficient breath for another try. It was not so much the physical exertion of the climbing that fatigued us, as the terrific wind pressure. It seemed to buffet the very energy from our bodies. Matinya and I had to keep low on our hands and knees to prevent ourselves being over-balanced by the force of the wind. When we were about half way up, and on the crest of the steepest saddle, Matinya, who had been afraid for some time, showed signs of refusing to go any further. He kept shouting that the wind would blow him over the edge, and, on occasions, I was inclined to agree with him. Even then, as I lay spread-eagled on the rock, gathering breath for yet another few yards, and looked up that ridge with nothing but open space on either side, I almost persuaded myself that the game was not worth the candle. But Matinya's fear had put me on my mettle. There was no turning back, I had to keep going.

Now and again we found shallow depressions, just deep enough to lie in and allow the furious icy blasts to sweep over the top of us. There we rested, the primitive man and myself, each somewhat fearful of the dangers around, but each moved by a vastly different urge—mine, that strange desire, belonging to my kind, to discover the unknown; his, not so clear—perhaps a sense of his duty as a host to me, his guest, for why else should he have faced such danger?

We finally reached the top, and took a much-needed rest. Matinya collected dry branches from a lone corkwood tree and lit a fire to thaw himself out, for he must have been very cold. Once, however, we were on the summit, and amid the deep gutters, we did not feel the wind again.

Uluru was well worth the struggle. It is a remarkable oval cavity in the bottom of one of the deep trough-like gutters which pour their waters over the side of the Rock. The water-hole is about thirty feet long, with almost perpendicular sides, except at the lower end. The position and vertical banks prevent the sun from shining on its surface for more than a few hours a day, reducing evaporation to a minimum. Those factors probably account for the permanent nature of the water-hole, the natives contending that even in the worst droughts Uluru never goes dry.

But of greater interest than its natural setting is the importance of Uluru in aboriginal mythology. For years I had known about the mighty struggles of the large snakes which, in 'Creation Times,' had taken place on its banks. The columns of rock lying near the water-hole were once the bodies of the Kunia (Carpet Snakes) which had rested there, and the deep gutters that scored the Rock from end to end were the tracks of those snakes as they travelled across the country. But the mythology of Uluru is not limited to the mighty happenings of the past, for in deep underground caverns, beneath the calm surface of the water, there still lives a Wonambi, a giant, many-coloured mythical serpent, whose original home was in the sky.

Matinya had good cause to remember that Wonambi. When climbing Ayers Rock previously, with Lauri and Tjundaga, he became thirsty and, without taking due precautions, drank from Uluru. The next day Matinya was sick with a feverish cold, and everyone was convinced that he had been attacked by the Wonambi. Old Tjalerina said that the illness was entirely Matinya's own fault, for he should have known that a fire lit at the edge of the water-hole would have driven the Wonambi back into his deep caverns.

On the day that we reached Uluru, Matinya, not going to be caught the second time, lit a smouldering fire near the water-hole as soon as we arrived; then he sat on the edge to watch for the movement of the water that would indicate when the snake had retreated to its underground home. So far as I could see, the water retained its mirror-like surface, but Matinya, satisfied that the fire had done its work, drank heavily, and suffered no ill-effects. Before returning I looked over the edge of the Rock, and saw Lauri and the aborigines like tiny specks, a thousand feet or more below. But although the descent was without incident, and my knees caused me no further trouble, it was a good two hours before we joined our companions on the plain.

When we had returned to Ayers Rock from Katatjuta on the previous evening, we had noticed that the aborigines did

not go back to their former sleeping places, but built new
windbreaks some distance away. Lauri and I naturally went
back to our old camp, and were about to light the fire
when Tjundaga came across, quite concerned, and warned us
against the danger of staying there. When Lauri asked the
reason, the camel-man explained that every windbreak more
than a few days old was inhabited by a *mamu*, or night-
dwelling spirit, and, unless we moved, the *mamu* in our
old windbreak would attack us when we were asleep and
make us ill.

Tjundaga's warning made clear to us why our aboriginal
companions did not return to their old camps, and why
those in permanent positions shift their windbreaks every
few days. Although the fear of the *mamu* is the cause of
that continual movement, it is possible that the belief grew
out of necessity, and that some wise old man originated the
legend to improve the camp hygiene. Conversely, the sickness associated with a filthy camp may have given rise to the
belief of the *mamu* in the breakwind.

We left for Mt. Conner and Ernabella early the following
morning. The icy cold wind that we had experienced at
Katatjuta and Ayers Rock continued throughout the whole
of the journey to Mt. Conner. Had I not wanted to save
my rapidly disintegrating boots, and incidentally my feet, I
would have walked to keep warm, but, as it was, I sat on
the back of a camel—and froze.

I had already journeyed over a thousand miles on camels,
and most of that over sandy, spinifex-covered deserts in
Central Australia. Those journeys would have been most
monotonous had it not been for the interesting things I saw
from my lofty seat. From there I had a new view, a bird's-
eye view of the spinifex and sand that passed beneath me.

Spinifex, or to give it its scientific name, *triodia*, covers
both the sandy desert and rough hills. It grows, like the
fairy mushroom rings, in circular clumps which propagate
outwards. One of the outer branches will bend downward,
take root, and start a fresh plant. That process goes on till
one sometimes sees a complete ring of grass, with an area of

clear ground in the centre. I was always on the look-out for a complete spinifex ring, though in all my journeyings I saw but two. It was like searching for a four-leafed clover.

Every leaf of a spinifex bush is armed with a point, sharper than the finest needle, so sharp indeed that it could penetrate even my heavy clothing. That the natives would not walk on a bush consciously is an indication of its prickliness, for the sole of an aboriginal's foot is as tough as the tread of a motor tyre. Nor would the camel-string travel in a straight line, but would leisurely wind its way in and out among the spinifex bushes. Everyone and everything, except the tiny creatures which made it their home, had as little as possible to do with that unfriendly desert dweller.

As the spinifex passed under my feet, day after day, week after week, I began to recognize the tracks made by those small creatures. I learned that in each clump, separated from the next by a space of clean sand, there lived families of mice, lizards, small marsupials and insects; self-contained communities, each intent on its own affairs, and seldom, if ever, troubling the others.

One day, as I idly watched from the back of my camel, I was struck by the resemblance of these little homes in the spinifex to those in a human suburban area. Each had its own inmates, each was separate from the next, so I called them Spinifex Town.

On cold mornings I would sometimes walk to gain a closer knowledge of the goings-on of those little people of Spinifex Town. It was a pleasant pastime. There I was moving in a world apart, a world of tiny creatures. The tracks left in the fine sand, as yet undisturbed by the day's breezes, told me so much of their movements that, although I never saw the inhabitants of that desert community, I knew about their doings, their habits and their characteristics.

First there were the mice, our little domestic mice, which seldom went straight from one home to another. They would creep beside a bunch of spinifex, and then, with a quick rush, break across the open space to seek shelter in a neighbour's house. The tiny marsupial mouse was almost as wary, but he often ventured further afield. Occasionally I saw where one had made an exploratory journey into the larger spaces for a tit-bit, or to meet a friend.

As the day became warmer the lizards started to wander. They were the sleep-a-beds, and never rose before the dew was off the grass. The little ones were as shy as the mice, but much faster in their movements. They made swift journeys from one place to another, pausing now and again in the shadow of a stick or a clump of grass to watch for intruders. They were so small, and so light, that their tracks were barely visible. The sleepy-lizards and goannas, on the other hand, moved deliberately from place to place, for who, except the eagle and man, could attack those giants of Spinifex Town?

The character of the birds, too, showed in their footmarks. The bombastic gait of the crow (*Corvus ceciloe*), that black robber of the Outback, was reflected in his swaggering tracks. The wild turkey (*Eupodis australis*) (alas, now almost extinct where white men and foxes roam) pursued his way in a straight line, like the gentleman he is. There was one little bird—I never found out who he was—who was such a busy-body. I could trace where he rushed here, stopped, changed his mind, and then tore off somewhere else. He hardly ever reached his destination before something diverted his attention, sending him in another direction. He must have been a very busy bird, and a tired one before the end of the day.

The rabbit was everywhere. The characteristic groups of little circular footmarks (three and one) showed his wanderings. How that little animal, who belongs to the greener places of the world, gathers food and water in that inhospitable country, where surface waters are non-existent, and rain-storms rare, was always a puzzle.

Then there were the insects, spiders, and all sorts of creeping things, which left evidence of their movements on the sandy page. I imagine they were a stupid crowd, and they must often have fallen prey to some watchful bird.

Tracks here, tracks there, on all sides of me, made by little creatures that knew not man, for seldom did that supreme egoist of creation come their way; yet each living in its own sphere, as much the work of the Creator as the visitor who watched their tracks and learned their ways from the back of a camel.

Although the aboriginal men had been lighting the spinifex to make smoke signals, so that Tjikaba would know that we were on the way to Mt. Conner, it was not until the middle of the third day that we saw an answering smoke on the horizon, which the men proclaimed was the work of Tjikaba. On reaching Anneri soak, however, we found that Nali, an aboriginal from the Musgrave Ranges, had lit that smoke signal, and not Tjikaba at all.

That was the only occasion on which I was able to check the accuracy of smoke signals. There has been a great deal of loose talk about aboriginal smoke signals. White men have told me some amazing stories on the subject, most of them involving the transmission of information of interest, not to the aborigines, but to the white man; the declaration of war; the death of some local person; or a bush tragedy. Usually, if the informant were pressed, he would finish up by admitting that he had heard the story from someone else, or had known the man who had seen the signals. One white miner, however, was more definite. He related a personal experience in which the aborigines had been able to tell him, a day in advance, of the approach of an unexpected party of visitors, the number, the name of the driver, and the make of the car—all by smoke signal! But a talk with the aborigines themselves made it quite clear to me that their method of signalling was so simple that the complex details could not have been transmitted.

Although the smoke signals throughout Central Australia are particularly simple, the deserts are ideal for their transmission. The country is level for a hundred miles or more, and the ubiquitous spinifex, when lit, gives a column of dense black smoke which can be seen for long distances. The aborigines, when hunting or travelling, continually light the spinifex to let the other family groups know of their movements. As the speed of those groups is seldom more than two to three miles an hour, and a smoke would be clearly visible at twenty miles, or even further, every family within that radius would be kept informed about the movements of the others; and as the number of aborigines living within that range would be small, the names of the people in each group could be estimated with a fair degree of certainty. So that, if the aborigines send messages in ways mysterious to the white man, it may be, after all, only the result of what is, to them, easy deduction from familiar circumstances.

Although the last word has yet to be written on the smoke signals of the aborigines, I am convinced that much which has been recorded about them is as exaggerated as the accounts of Indian rope tricks, hoop snakes and mulga wireless.

". . . his place was taken by an even more delightful aborigine, named Jabiaba."
(Page 110.)

". . . the aborigines do not drink from the main source but from a hole dug in the sand alongside." *(Page 118.)*

Chapter XV

The Burial Ceremony

WHEN WE RETURNED TO Ernabella we found that the disbanding of a ceremonial group, known colloquially as the Red Ochre party, had temporarily increased the aboriginal population four-fold.

Little is known about those curious ceremonies, which are carried out in turn by one tribe after another, across the continent. Dr. Roth, in 1893, saw one in Queensland, the Titjinalla, which was performed by the tribes in the Lake Eyre basin seven years later, and which reached northern Central Australia in 1903. The Red Ochre party travelled even more slowly, for six years later I met it again at Areyonga, in the western Macdonnell Ranges, less than a hundred and fifty miles from the Musgrave Ranges.

A Red Ochre party consists of a group of patriarchs, the Kaliurana, who are in charge of the camp and the ceremonies, and a number of men and women who are passing through the rituals. When the people of one group have completed their initiation, which occupies some weeks, they return to their homes, and their places are taken by others, already chosen by the Kaliurana. The new arrivals and their families are given instructions as to the procedures of initiation and codes of behaviour, before they are admitted to the grounds of the Red Ochre party. Once inside, the women take their part in the songs and dances peculiar to themselves, whilst the men pass through a secret initiation ritual, in the climax of which a number of sacred objects are displayed—stone *tjurunga*[1] from the Macdonnell Ranges, baler shell ornaments from Cape York, and pearl shells from north-western Australia. After this initiation, the men, when not gathering food, spend their days performing ceremonies associated with Milbili, the Goanna ancestor, and their evenings either in the

[1] Engraved sacred stones.

social life of the camp or in dancing or singing the non-secret ceremonies.

Each Red Ochre party lasts from four to six months, or until every man and woman in the neighbourhood has been initiated. The participants then return to their tribal lands, and the ceremony is passed to an adjacent tribe.

The gathering is probably more social than ceremonial in function. Both men and women live within the camp, mix freely, and participate at least in the non-secret dances. One of the fundamental laws of a Red Ochre camp, which emphasizes its social nature, insists that univeral friendliness and goodwill must, at all times, prevail. Any infringement is met by immediate expulsion and, later, punishment.

While we were at Ernabella we did little else but load the camels with fresh supplies, read and answer our letters, and chose the aborigines, including some from the Red Ochre party, to accompany us on the westerly journey. We were sorry that some tribal business prevented old Tjalerina from coming with us, as both Lauri and I had grown fond of the old man. But as luck would have it, his place was taken by an even more delightful aborigine, named Jabiaba, who, as a born mimic and wit, was a favourite of everyone.

The whole of the aboriginal population of Ernabella left at the same time as ourselves to attend the final burial rituals of Namana, a man who had died some three months previously. As we were anxious to learn more about the ceremonies and beliefs of burial, and as Owellinna water, their destination, was on our track, we decided to accompany them.

For two days we travelled south, with the red-brown Musgraves rising on either side of us. The flats between the ranges were covered with a sea of flaxen-white mulga-grass and dotted with low eucalypts, stunted corkwoods, and, occasionally, the bright-green, pendulous-foliaged iron-wood trees. Here and there an island of sunburnt rocks pushed its way through the grassy surface to provide a home for the native pines (*Callitris* sp.) and fig-trees (*Ficus platypoda*).

Owellinna spring, our destination, is a stream of crystal clear water that flows from an opening in the hillside, ripples its way over a stony creek bottom, only to lose itself in a bed of sand a few miles from its source. Lauri and I pitched our tents nearby, for that was the first, and only time, that we heard the pleasant sound of running water during the whole of our desert journey. About a quarter of a mile distant, the aborigines had established a camp in readiness for the coming burial rituals.

We spent most of the following day gathering information, not only about customs and beliefs of burial, but also about *kuranita*, that mysterious life essence which permeates the whole of nature. Jabiaba, our chief informant, explained how, before *tjukurita*, or 'Creation Times,' the world was a huge plain, dry, featureless, and entirely devoid of life. Then came the *tjukurita* people, immense, semi-human creatures, themselves stores of *kuranita*, who created the countryside as the aborigines know it today. Everything that was made in *tjukurita* times, the rocks, the water-courses, the trees and all living creatures, including man, was permeated with that vital essence, *kuranita*, whose presence means life, and whose absence death.

When one or another of those ancestral beings died, their bodies, transformed into some natural feature, usually a rock or a tree, became concentrated masses of their own life essence, or *kuranita*. A rock, once the body of a goanna, is today full of the *kuranita* of goannas; a particular tree, the transformed body of a carpet snake, is full of the *kuranita* of carpet snakes, and so on. The places where those ancestors died are known to the natives as *pulkarin*. They are localities at which the aborigines assemble, at certain times of the year, to increase, by appropriate chants and rituals, the supply of plants and animals required for food. Thus, the ceremony at a kangaroo *pulkarin* will make the kangaroos reproduce more freely, that at a grass-seed *pulkarin* will make the grass more fertile, and that at a fig-tree *pulkarin* will make the tree bear more fruit.

The amount of *kuranita* possessed by anything is in direct relation to its own vitality. Rocks and grass have little, trees have about the same amount as each other, the emu has more than the wild turkey, the kangaroo more than the wallaby, the man more than the woman, and the medicine-man most of all.

The *kuran* of the newly-dead is greatly feared. Aborigines, unaware that death is the result of natural causes, believe that all such calamities are due to the malignant magic of some enemy. Therefore, the spirit of the dead man, angry because it has been robbed of life, takes every opportunity of avenging itself upon its living associates.

The whole pattern of the burial ceremonies is based on that fear of the spirit of the newly dead, and the precautions necessary to protect the living from its malignant power. At the moment of death, all the immediate relatives flee from the camp to a distant locality, leaving their belongings behind them, to mislead the spirit of the dead man into thinking that they have only gone hunting, and will return. Those who bury the dead man make him warm and comfortable in his grave, so that his spirit will be less inclined to wander, while everyone mourns loud and long to appease the spirit, and so reduce its enmity. The *kuran* of the dead man, longing for human companionship, sits on a small mound at the head of the grave, beside the dead fires in the deserted camp awaiting the return of its human friends, or roams the bush in search of them.

About three months after the death, two medicine men, accompanied by the relatives of the deceased, travel to the grave, capture the *kuran*, and place it in the body of a living person. This ritual serves a double purpose: it gives the spirit a new home, so that it will no longer be a danger to the community, and, by providing the host with an extra *kuran*, endows him with greater power and vitality. It is, important, however, that the *kuran* should be given to some-one of the same age: a child's to a child, a youth's to a youth, an adult's to an adult, and an old man's to an old man. If the *kuran* of a young man were placed in the body of one

(a) Aborigine with spear and spear-thrower carrying newly-killed kangaroo. *(Page 120.)*

(b) "The aboriginal method of cooking the euro could scarcely have been simpler." *(Page 121.)*

AN ABORIGINAL WOMAN WINNOWING GRASS-SEED
"The aboriginal women are the more reliable of the food gatherers . . . ."
(Page 122.)

much older, the young spirit, with its greater vitality, would wear the older man out. Conversely, if the spirit of an old man were placed in the body of a youth, the old *kuran* would drain so heavily on the younger man for sustenance that he would become listless, tired, and of little use at hunting or food-gathering. If, however, the *kuran* were given to a person of the same age, the additional vitality would help him to live a little longer.

So far as we could ascertain, the desert people have no conception of a future life. The apparent absence of that belief was not surprising, for the spirit of the dead man, being always placed in a living body of the same age, must become progressively older, until, at senility, the *kuran* is so weak and harmless that the medicine man will even not trouble to go to the grave to capture it. The frail, tiny *kuran* is allowed to wander round the bush until it is destroyed by some *mamu* or night-dwelling spirit.

The aborigines had assembled at Owellinna to capture the *kuran*, and perform the final burial rites of the dead man, Namana. A small party, including two medicine men, were to leave at sunrise, travel to the grave, about fifteen miles distant, and return next day. Although Tjundaga, Jabiaba and Moanya were forbidden to attend, Lauri and I were allowed to accompany the party.

The next morning, as soon as we arrived at the main camp, some twenty men and women set off at a run to their destination, while the hundred or more who remained behind threw themselves on the ground, and broke into loud and continuous lamentations. To see the huddled, sorrowing people, with their naked bodies shining in the low morning light, and to hear the massed high-pitched lament from a hundred throats, was an experience so strange and unusual that I seemed to be in another age, far back in time.

We followed the travelling aborigines through a deep gorge, heavily overgrown with ti-tree, the sound of the mourning people growing fainter and fainter in the distance. As we pushed our way through that thick growth, with the all-pervading pungent odour of crushed leaves in

J

our nostrils, and the dusky forms of the native people appearing and disappearing in the gloom of the dense scrub, that earlier sense of detachment and isolation was intensified. It was not that I was afraid or lonely, although we scarcely could have been more separated from our kind; it was simply that the experiences through which I was passing were so dissociated, so apart from ordinary living, that I had no link with them. I was a stranger, I was an outsider, I did not belong.

After about a mile, the gorge became lower, allowing the sunlight to fall on the steep walls and the gum trees that grew at their base. In the low light of the new day those trees were a lovely sight, their trunks smooth, cream-coloured, and rounded like the limbs of young girls.

For the first time I was able to take stock of our companions, particularly the two medicine-men; one was tall and dignified, broad of shoulder and slender of limb, a friendly man with kindly eyes; the other, young, slight and graceful, the gracefulness that belongs to a cat or a panther. The elder son of Matinya, a boy about twelve, also attracted my attention. He walked always with the men, imitating them in every action, carrying proudly in his right hand a diminutive spear and spearthrower that someone had made for him. It will be a happy day for that little chap when he is admitted to the ranks of manhood.

In the middle of the afternoon we tied the camels to some mulga trees, and followed the aborigines, who, with branches in their hands, were running toward the grave. Every now and again they stopped to call out, in a high-pitched voice, to let the *kuran* of Namana know that they were coming. After about two miles of alternately running and calling out, the party reached the camp where the man had died. Personal belongings were lying everywhere, thrown down by the aborigines in their headlong flight to escape the angry and malignant spirit of the newly-dead man. While the men and the women swept round the wind-breaks and dead camp-fires to hunt the spirit of Namana back to his grave, the medicine men, who are the only ones who can see the *kuran*, preceded the main party to capture the *kuran*, as it made its way to the head of the grave to await the arrival of its old friends and associates.

The elder medicine man told me afterwards that the spirit of Namana was not at the grave, but nobody seemed to know why. He admitted that the relatives had been in too great a hurry; they should have made smoke signals, and camped for a day or two. Then, if the *kuran* had been visiting the birthplace of Namana, it would, on seeing the smoke signal, and knowing the reason for it, have travelled across the country to the grave. The medicine man said that more attempts should have been made to attract, or to frighten, the spirit to the burial place, so that it could have continued to live in someone else. A *kuran* should not be doomed to wander in a disembodied state until it was captured by one of the spirits of darkness.

When the main party reached the grave, they stuffed branches into the crevices between the logs which covered the burial place, filling the spaces that remained with loose sand. The aborigines then took handfuls of the grave earth, smelt it, and rubbed it over their legs, for the odour made them strong, and the rubbing prevented their legs from getting tired on the long journeys. The party then set out toward our camels, first visiting their old camp to collect carrying dishes, grinding stones and other valuables they had left behind.

Lauri and I had our meal while the aborigines cooked the kangaroos they had caught on the outward journey. I went to bed soon afterwards, for the long run to the grave with the aborigines had made me particularly tired. As I lay in my sleeping-bag, idly listening to the activities nearby, a chance remark from Lauri suddenly made me realize our exceptional position. There we were, unarmed, surrounded by primitive people, all of whom were strangers, they unable to speak our language, we, theirs but poorly. Yet we were in no more danger in that camp than we would have been in our own homes, and less than in the city streets. We had no need to fear the aborigines, for they are an essentially peaceful people, and only retaliated after continuous ill-treatment or oppression. It may be taken as a maxim that any white man who, at the present, is attacked by the natives, has earned his punishment many times before he receives it.

The next morning, when we started for home, the women who were carrying the children looked so tired that Lauri and I took their babies from them, one at a time, and carried them with us on the camels. The little mites, who knew only kindness in their short lives, stayed with us for hours, contented and unafraid.

By the middle of the afternoon we were within sight of the camp at Owellinna. From the back of the camel, I could see the aborigines lying close together on the ground, crying softly. The returning party again collected branches, and, calling out in the same high-pitched voices they had used at the grave, walked slowly forward, and cast the branches on the mourning people.

Instantly pandemonium broke loose. The sounds of mourning rose to a high-pitched wail; the men sobbed heart-brokenly; twenty or thirty women, screaming loudly, were either throwing themselves on the ground with dull, sickening thuds, or vehemently lacerating their scalps with digging sticks. It was a scene of uncontrolled grief and mass hysteria. Yet, in contrast to that unhappy, sorrowing throng were two rows of men, lying face downwards, their bodies rigid, their arms locked about each other, and hands tightly clenched. Then came the most curious and unexplainable part of the whole strange ceremony, something which suggested a possible belief in a future life: the resurrection of the 'dead' man. The living men disentangled the stiff, rigid bodies, one by one, turning them face upwards, bending the trunks, unclenching the hands, vigorously rubbing the bodies and limbs, and roughly pulling the ears. Slowly each 'dead' man came to life; his body and limbs lost their rigidity, his hands relaxed, his eyes opened, until eventually he sat up and mourned with the rest. As the ceremony progressed, more and more 'dead' men were brought to life; the sounds of the mourning died down; the women throwing themselves

". . . we saw many groups of the rare desert grass-tree (Xanthorrhoea thorntonii)."
(Page 130.)

WATERING CAMELS, PILTADI

". . . every drop had to be carried down in buckets and poured into a tarpaulin stretched over a bowl-shaped depression."   *(Page 133.)*

on the ground became fewer and fewer, until only one figure remained. She was the mother of Namana. Her yellow, ochre-covered body, streaked with the blood that flowed from her wounded scalp, was so exhausted she could scarcely raise herself to a standing position to cast herself down once more.

Most curious of all was the behaviour of the children. Amid all the wailing and hysteria, the girls, undisturbed by the turmoil beside them, played quietly at some childish pastime; and the excited laughter of the boys, entirely engrossed in their spear and disc games, mingled strangely with the lamentations of their elders. There, side by side, we saw the two extremes of emotion, the grief and frenzy of those at the burial ceremony, and the uninhibited laughter of children at play.

Chapter XVI

The Journey to Oparinna

THE NEXT DAY, WITH MOST of the aborigines from the burial ceremony, we reached Erliwunyawunya, a large water catchment, picturesquely situated between high, red cliffs. As the country had been without rain for months, the water was foul and green, for Erliwunyawunya is only a rock-hole, not a spring. However, as the party faced a long, dry stage, we had to take and be thankful for whatever water the Fates provided, good or bad. But with the water in such a foul state, every drop had to be boiled before Lauri and I could drink it, not so much to improve its unpleasant taste, as to eliminate all danger of disease. The aborigines do not seem to be affected by impure waters, though I have noticed that, whenever there is a sandy edge to the supply, such as at Erliwunyawunya, the natives do not drink from the main source, but from a hole dug in the sand alongside; a sound practice, as the water seeping in, in, being well filtered, is comparatively clean.

While the canteens were being replenished, we saw a hunting party come in, the men following each other in single file. The two leaders each carried a euro (*Macropus robustus*) on his head, and the others had in their hands either the intestines, bundled into neat parcels, or just their spears and spear-throwers.

The euro, really a hill kangaroo, is not an easy animal to capture in its native habitat; its rusty-red colour so matches the rocks that it is difficult to see; its keen hearing, which detects the slightest sound, makes it hard to approach; and the speed with which it can hop from one rocky foot-hold to another makes it almost impossible for either man or dog to run it down. But the southern Musgrave Ranges, with their isolated hills, each separated from the others by grassy flats, are an excellent hunting ground for euros. The creatures, shunning the open plains where their colour makes them conspicuous, always choose the shortest route across the flats which separate one hill from the next, routes which, in the course of time, have often become well-defined tracks.

By the use of those tracks, the aborigines have developed a system of hunting, perfected by generations of experiment and practice. The method is simple. The spearmen, concealed behind trees or low bush shelters, are posted along the path chosen for the day's hunt, whilst the remainder of the men, who constitute the beaters, start at the distant end of one hill and, lighting the spinifex as they go, drive the game toward the spearmen. The euros travel ahead of the fire until they reach the nearest point to the next hill. Their only way of escape is along the path that crosses the intervening flat. There is apparent safety in front, and danger behind. The native waits until the euro is comparatively close before he launches his spear. It is a lucky beast that gets away. Even if the spear does not kill, it so retards the animal that it is easily captured.

The kangaroo of the plains (*Macropus rufus*) can be speared from a hide in a similar manner, but the procedure of driving is different, for the kangaroo shuns the hills as much as the euro does the plains. Nevertheless, when the animals are travelling to and from their feeding grounds, they often follow well-defined pads. Several hunters take up their positions on one of these tracks, while the others quietly disturb the feeding kangaroos and shepherd them in the right direction. A spearman is able to stand in almost clear view to throw his weapon, for the kangaroo, when escaping from his enemies, concentrates his attention on the path in front, and the danger behind.

The best exhibition of hunting that we saw, however, was on the day that Tilbukuna stalked and killed a kangaroo single-handed. He had sighted the creature feeding on a plain, open except for a few corkwood and mulga trees. Signalling to us to keep quiet, Tilbukuna made a wide circuit until he was down-wind. Then, taking advantage of every tree and shrub, he crept towards the unsuspecting animal until a hundred yards of open plain, devoid of cover, separated him from his quarry. The hunter waited until the animal put his head down to feed. Then, with spear poised on his spear-thrower, he stepped boldly into the open, and with no movement, save that of his legs, walked slowly towards the kangaroo. As soon as the creature raised its head, the hunter 'froze,' and remained as immovable as the rocks on the hillside until the animal started its meal afresh. Slowly and patiently the stalk went on, the native moving up a few steps, pausing when the animal looked up, a few more steps, another pause, and so on, until less than a chain separated the hunter from the hunted.

When the animal put its head down, for what was to be its last mouthful of grass, Tilbukuna stiffened, transferred his weight to his back foot, then, using the whole momentum of his body, launched his spear. The creature bounded away in fright and pain, for the spear had pierced its ribs. The chase was short and the end certain.

Tilbukuna immediately disembowelled the kangaroo, closing the small cut in the abdomen with a pointed twig and a binding of intestine. He then bent the body practically double by disjointing the hind legs and tying them and the tail to the forepaws. That made a particularly neat parcel, which balanced well on Tilbukuna's head, the best way to carry such a load, for a full-sized kangaroo weighs up to eighty pounds. Naturally, as the kangaroo cannot always be captured near the camp, the natives often have to bring them in long distances. If several men are present, the beast may be cooked on the spot, and the load distributed, otherwise the body is removed intact.

Although I have seen many kangaroos brought in, the only time that I could make sure how far one had been carried was in the deserts of Western Australia. Our party had asked an aborigine to get us a kangaroo for food. In due time the native returned, threw the body on the ground, and left without a word. A few days later we passed the spot where the hunter had disembowelled the creature, and found out that the distance was over five miles from our tents.

The aboriginal method of cooking the euro could scarcely be simpler. At Erliwunyawunya, the natives dug a shallow trench in the ground, filled it with light branches, and set them on fire. While the fire was burning down, the men prepared the animal for the oven, first by throwing it on the flames, to scorch the fur from its body, then by cutting off the feet of the hind legs and the tail. The feet and the tail were later put at the bottom of the trench so that they would be better cooked. By the time the euro was ready for the oven, the fire had burned down. The embers were then raked out, the euro placed on its back in the trench and covered with hot sand and ashes. The carcase was left to cook for about an hour, certainly not long for a beast weighing fifty pounds. However, I have seen an eighty-pound kangaroo taken from the oven after twenty minutes. It was no exaggeration to say that the flesh was under-done.

Although the aboriginal method of cooking is primitive, it has points in its favour. The flesh of the animal, being enclosed in its own skin, is entirely protected from the contamination of flies, human beings, dust and ashes; also, the preliminary scorching, when the fur is removed, so hardens the skin that it becomes a complete cooking vessel—a stone-age men's casserole—which retains all the body juices.

On the day that we were at Erliwunyawunya, I noticed that the men who carried the carcases did not take part either in the cooking or the sharing out of the meat. At the time that did not seem particularly odd, for everyone had helped in the capturing of the euro. It was later, when Tilbukuna speared the kangaroo single-handed, that I first learned the principles of the food distribution system. He brought the kangaroo into the camp, laid it at the feet of old Jabiaba, sat down by the fire, and apparently took no further interest in the matter. Jabiaba cooked the beast, gave the least desirable parts of the body to Tilbukuna, reserved the dainties, such as the liver, kidneys and fat, for himself and portioned out the rest of the meat, even the best joints, to the other members of the group.

That method of division appeared to be universal; whether the game was large or small, or the participants men or women, the hunter neither cooked his catch nor had any say in the manner in which it was shared. In the long run, however, each person received an equal portion of the food, for the hunter of one day would be the cook or recipient on another.

There appears to be, however, a much wiser purpose behind the custom than the mere distribution of food. The government of the tribe is in the hands of the old men, and it is they who have the power to make decisions and ensure their enforcement. Were the skilled hunters, who are generally young, allowed to apportion their own catch, they could, by bartering their game for privileges and power, upset the authority of the old men, and so, the social balance of the tribe. But under aboriginal law, the successful hunter, young or old, can gain no advantage. His skill is of more value to the tribe than to himself; his only return is the joy of achievement, and the approbation of his fellows.

Although, no doubt, there are more complex rules governing this custom than appear on the surface, the system was quite stable, for there was never any argument or dissatisfaction about the food sharing. Neither was there any discrimination in the amount of food given to men or women, though many writers on aboriginal life say the husband keeps the best for himself and gives the rest to his wife.

But there is a definite division of food-gathering between the men and the women, necessitated somewhat by the functions of the two sexes. The men hunt the larger creatures, the kangaroos, the emus, the wallabies, and the big lizards, and their hunting involves unrestricted movement, as well as long, tiring journeys. The women, on the other hand, laden with the children and the camp gear, travel from water-hole to water-hole, by a comparatively direct route, gathering the more accessible foods, the grass seeds, fruits, small reptiles and wood grubs. The aboriginal women are the more reliable of the food gatherers. Many days the men return empty-handed, for the desert animals are wary and difficult to catch, but the women always bring in some food; at times it is not much, nor particularly tasty, but it is at least sufficient to keep the family going until the luck of the men changes.

The food of the aborigines is varied, and is, from the standpoint of nutrition, well balanced. Their meats range from the larger creatures, kangaroos, emus, to wood grubs and even termites; their bread is made from the seeds of the various grasses, mulga, and other acacias; and at different seasons of the year wild fruits, such as plums, figs, peaches and desert tomatoes, as well as a number of green fleshy-leafed plants, and tree blossoms, add variety to their diet. Though the desert does not always yield an abundance, the natives do not suffer from deficiency diseases until they attach themselves to our civilization, to be fed on white flour, tea, sugar and little else.

We had planned to travel direct from Erliwunyawunya to Piltadi, a rock-hole on the eastern end of the Mann Ranges, a journey which would have involved a five days' dry stage. But so many of the aborigines from the burial service accompanied us that we had to abandon the scheme, for we could not carry sufficient water to last such a party two, let alone five days. So we decided to follow a line of small springs which would lead us to Oparinna water, on the western end of the Musgrave Ranges, and from there to move on to Piltadi.

It took us three days to reach Oparinna, for much of the track through the rough ranges was slow and difficult. The first night, at Ipudulkana spring, which is in a small gorge, was the most uncomfortable that I have ever spent in Central Australia. There were aborigines, dogs and camp-fires everywhere, some of the fires being within a few yards of us. The choking smoke, the hordes of marauding dogs, and the ceaseless chatter of people (for they seemed to have stayed up all night) made me pleased indeed to see the first signs of dawn. Fortunately, a number of aborigines remained at Ipudulkana, and an equal number at Weeloo

soak, which we passed in the middle of the afternoon; so
that by the time we camped on the second evening we
had less than twenty aborigines with us, most of them old
acquaintances.

On our journey to Oparinna we passed several interesting
places associated with the aboriginal myths; one belonging to
a wounded euro which was endeavouring to escape from its
enemies; another dealing with a sky legend, where the
Kunkarunkara women, now the Pleiades, came to earth to
collect food, but were pursued by Nirunya, the man of
Orion; and yet another, not far from Oparinna, where the
aborigines assemble to perform food increase ceremonies
which will make the snakes multiply more freely.

Some time during the journey from Ernabella, Numidi
had acquired a stock of red ochre, part of which she had
traded to Nibiana, the wife of the camel-man, for a dirty,
ragged dress. I had had a great deal of trouble in the cine
photographs with that dress, for if anything important was
happening, Numidi, in that awful rag, was sure to be there.
I did not say anything to her about it, for after all it was
her dress, but made plans to buy it from her somehow or
another.

One morning, as I was writing up my diary, and Numidi
was standing alongside, watching and making occasional
remarks, I asked her if she would give me her dress. She,
of course, refused. Dipping into a case beside me, I brought
out a double handful of boiled sweets, tipped a packet of
dried apricots on top, and said:

'*Woma* (sweets or sugar) for *raga* (dress).'

'*Wia, wia* (No, no),' said Numidi.

I doubled the size of the pile of sweets, and added a
carton of dried prunes.

'*Raga* (dress) for *woma, bulka* (sugar, plenty),' I said.

'*Wia, wia* (No, no),' said Numidi again, but, I thought,
not so definitely as before.

I kept on increasing the pile until Numidi succumbed,
took off her dress, gave it to me, and walked off with her
wooden dish overflowing with dainties.

"The Fates were on our side, for Piltadi still held two to three hundred gallons of black, putrid water." *(Page 133.)*

"That Wonambi is now a curiously-shaped blood-wood tree, . . . The dead limb is the digging stick . . . the lumps and excrescences on the trunk, the body of the woman . . . ." *(Page 135.)*

The other women were pleased about the exchange. Perhaps Numidi had been 'lording it' over them; but even if she had not done so, having a dress, when the rest of the women were without them, made her a person to be envied. So, by my wealth, I was able to restore a social balance, as well as to remove an ever-present danger to the photographic records.

Of course, the sweets did not last long, and Numidi was too astute a lady to accept the loss of her dress without making some effort to regain it. She tried all her feminine wiles to get it back; offered me her carrying dish, her digging-stick, and her precious stock of red ochre; she even went so far as to enlist the help of Nibiana, who, being able to speak English, could plead a better case. But I remained adamant and refused to return the garment to the lady until, some weeks later, we were on our homeward journey.

But Numidi did not want that dress to cover up her nakedness. She was unaware that clothes were required for that purpose; in fact, before the aborigines are spoiled by close contact with our civilization, they have no self-consciousness about nudity. Still, though their culture gives them little opportunity for personal decoration, and consequent self-pride, the aborigines are, after all, human beings and, like ourselves, will use any means to gain social approval. Hence Numidi's desire for that dress.

Chapter XVII

The Rain-making Ceremony

WE EXPECTED THE NEXT objective, the Mann Ranges, to be the highlight of our research, for the whole area is rich in mythological stories. As we had already collected much information on the mythology of the Mann Ranges, and had persuaded a number of aborigines belonging to that country to accompany us, we felt well equipped to carry out an unusually good piece of work.

But, 'the best-laid schemes o' mice and men gang aft agley.' On the morning following our arrival at Oparinna, two aboriginal girls, returning from the Western Australian border with some camels belonging to a trespassing dogger, brought in the bad news that all except one of the water-holes in the Mann Ranges were dry, and that one, Piltadi, was so full of dead dogs and kangaroos that the girls had to clean it out before they could get water for their camels. So, as we could carry barely sufficient water to last our party as far as Piltadi, let alone the eighty miles the length of the Mann Ranges, we either had to turn back from Oparinna or alter our plans.

After a long talk, Lauri and I decided to continue the journey, but to reduce the string from twelve to five camels; we would also leave all but two of our informants behind, and travel direct to Piltadi on a water ration limited to three pints a day until we were sure of the conditions ahead. If Piltadi were dry we would return immediately, for by then the camels would be in need of water; if Piltadi still held water we should use it as a base, and travel out as far as possible.

We spent all that day re-sorting our supplies, for a string of five camels—two riding, one pack, one box and one water camel—leaves little room for excess baggage. The final party consisted of Tjundaga, the camel-man, Moanya, Jabiaba, Lauri and myself. Naturally there was a great deal of talk about our altered plans, for the aborigines wanted to accompany us to the Mann Ranges, their homeland. Many of them had asked me direct to take them, others through Tjundaga or Nibiana, but to do so was out of the question, for a larger party meant greater and unnecessary risks.

Then a group of old men, headed by Tilbukuna, came across to my tent and suggested in their quaint way that I could safely take the whole party with me, because they had decided to make rain to help me out of my difficulties. That was especially good news, for, although I had no confidence in their rain-making ability, I was glad of the opportunity to learn about both the beliefs and the procedures of rain-making.

The central point of the rain-making rituals was a disc of pearl shell. It was one of the many that pass along a remarkable trade route, which starts on the coast of north-western Australia and finishes on the shores of the Great Australian Bight, over two thousand miles distant. At their source the shells are full-sized, often engraved with curious angular-meander designs; but as they move further south and take on the function of rain-making, the continual rubbing of their edges in the rain-making rituals so reduces their size that, by the time they reach the south coast of Australia, they are little larger than florins.[1] On some of them, however, traces of the designs of north-western Australia still show whence they came. It must be a long time before a pearl-shell ornament from north-western Australia finally reaches the southern edge of the continent.

Although the aboriginal men have no real knowledge about the origin of those ornaments, their belief that the shells come from a place, called by them Tapidji, where dangerous lizards (obviously crocodiles) live in the water, and eat people, is not far from the truth. Their belief also teaches them that the medicine-men of Tapidji catch the *ringili* (pearl-shells) as they swim around in the water, transfixing them with a specially thin spear. The shells are

[1] See Mountford, C. P., and Harvey, Alison, 1938, *Records, S. Aust. Museum*, Vol. VI, No. 2, pp. 115-135, "A Survey of Aboriginal Pearl and Baler Shell Ornaments."

then placed in the sun to harden. The wound caused by the spear becomes the hole on the edge of the shell through which is threaded the suspension cord. Tilbukuna, who was in charge of the rain-making rituals, told us on one occasion he had tried to reach Tapidji, so that he could capture some *ringili* for himself, but had not been able to do so.

The rain-making ceremony is based on the belief that the *ringili* (the pearl-shell) is impregnated with the *kuranita* (life essence) of water, and that the *kuranita*, when projected into the air, forms clouds which, under the stimulus provided by the chants and rituals, grow larger and larger, until rain falls. Tilbukuna said jokingly that he would have to be careful how he carried out the rituals, otherwise he would make so much rain that it would wash the camels away. But Jabiaba was quick to assure me that he could stop the rain at any time by sprinkling ashes on the *ringili*, wrapping it with fur string, and burying it beside a camp fire.

During the ceremony, which took place out of sight of the women, a number of men chanted the songs whilst Tilbukuna performed the rituals. He first squirted a stream of chewed native tobacco (*Nicotiana* sp.) on a flat stone, then rubbed the edge of the *ringili* across it, sucking the shell at intervals and spitting into the sky. Leaving the line of chanting men, Tilbukuna then walked across an open flat, lightly touching the tops of the mulga grass with the pearl-shell. Returning to the ceremonial ground, he put a mixture of blood and crushed grass on the flat stone, and continued, alternately, to rub the shell across the stone, or suck it and spit into the air. At the completion of the rituals, the pearl-shell was hung, by its suspension string, on a low mulga tree, so that it could swing freely.

The significance of the various phases of the ceremony is of more than ordinary interest, and illustrates the method by which the aborigines believe they can control the forces of nature by sympathetic magic. The chewed tobacco smelt like rain, the sucking extracted the *kuranita* of rain, and the spitting projected it into the sky. Each droplet then became

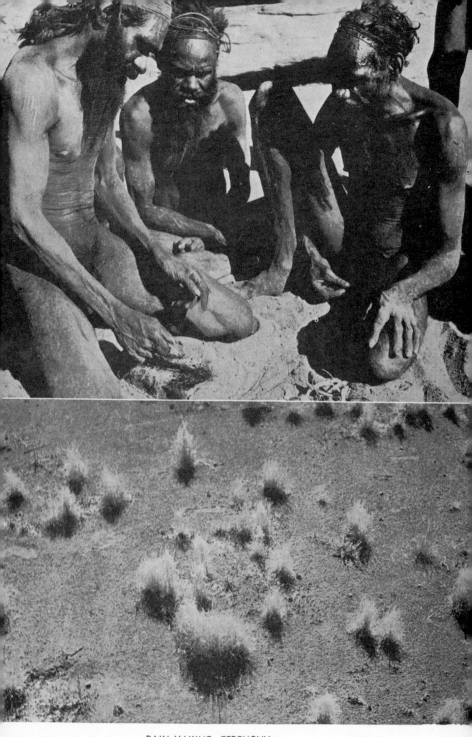

RAIN-MAKING CEREMONY

(a) Tibukuna rubbing pearl-shell ornament across a flat stone to extract the kuranita (life essence) of rain. *(Page 127.)*

(b) ". . . the creamy-whiteness of the mulga-grass resembles young clouds." *(Page 129.)*

"The desert kurrajong (Brachychiton gregorii) . . . is one of the most beautiful of the desert trees." *(Page 129.)*

the nucleus of a cloud, which grew rapidly under the influence of the appropriate chants. As the creamy-whiteness of the mulga grass resembled young clouds, the touching of that grass with the *ringili* had the effect of making the embryo clouds in the sky, formed by the drops of water *kuranita,* to run together, whilst the swinging of the pearl-shell on the end of its cord beckoned the rain to the place of the ceremony.

The next morning we set out for the Mann Ranges, five men and five camels, two of the men, at least, wondering what the future had in store. For most of the three days we travelled through interminable mulga scrubs and spinifex, though the monotony was relieved somewhat by occasional outcrops of boulders, associated in legendary stories with the large lizards, the emus, and the triad of ancestors who always moved together, the kangaroo, euro and night-owl.

On the second day we battled with an exhausting, hot wind, and before the morning was half over I was longing for my midday drink. One can feel very thirsty on three pints of water a day, particularly if the food lacks moisture; but as my tongue and mouth did not become dry (they had done so previously when I was short of water), I concluded that my body, though craving for more, was getting enough water to keep it going. I felt convinced that, in an emergency, the meagre allowance of three pints a day would suffice. Had we been travelling in summer, we certainly should have had to increase the ration, or adopt the common-sense aboriginal method of resting quietly during the day, travelling only at night.

In the middle of the afternoon we reached a belt of vegetation composed entirely of desert kurrajong, low mallee and spinifex, a refreshing sight after the mulga scrubs, which, especially if one is tired, seem unchanging, just one dark-foliaged tree after another.

The desert kurrajong (*Brachychiton gregorii*) with its smooth, light-green trunks, and symmetrical heads of lush-green foliage, is one of the most beautiful of the desert trees. As these kurrajong trees are comparatively rare, being found

K

only in the arid country far removed from water, few bot-
anists have had the pleasure of seeing them. Wherever those
trees grow they are associated with, and often surrounded by,
a ring of low mallee. Either one of the species is parasitical
upon the other, or they have formed one of those strange
partnerships that so often occur in nature, each supplying
what the other lacks. The kurrajongs are an excellent source
of food for the aborigines. They cook the young shoots,
strip off the bark and eat the sweet sapwood, grind the seeds
into flour, and, in an emergency, can get water by uprooting
a small tree, burning the foliage, and catching the fluid in
their wooden dishes as it drips from the taproot.

A little before reaching the kurrajong belt we saw many
groups of the desert grass-tree (*Xanthorrhoea thorntonii*),
which is even more rare than the kurrajong, but the grass-
trees do not fit into the landscape like the kurrajong; on the
other hand, they looked so out of place that it was easy to
imagine they had wandered from the hill country and been
unable to find their way back.

Toward evening it seemed as if the magic of the rain-
maker was starting to work, for there were many clouds,
broken cumulus, with a background of cirrus. I watched
them with pleasure, picturing a shape here and there, enjoying their grouping and the play of light and shade on their
ever-changing patterns. The Mann Ranges were due west,
and, under the conditions of that late afternoon, were in
colour a violet-blue, especially when some shaft of sunlight
broke through the clouds and fell across the steep gullies.
The clouds then turned all golden-edged, whilst now and
again a beam of light spread fan-wise to the zenith. It
seemed that Nature was endeavouring to provide some
recompense for a disagreeable day, because, that evening, the
western sky was transformed into a blaze of colour which
slowly faded into the mystery of night.

After all, we did not reach Piltadi on the third evening,
for Tjundaga and the other aborigines, wishing to give
me a surprise, decided to go to Ungata water-hole, which,
according to Moanya, who owned the country, never went

dry. When I noticed that they had altered the course, I was annoyed that they should have done so without consulting me, for we could ill afford to gamble with time, but I gave in without comment, for Moanya should know his own tribal area, and besides the aborigines were as anxious as Lauri and I to have a good drink.

Not far from Ungata, Moanya pointed out a number of long stones of rectangular section which were lying about on the ground. Each piece of stone represented the *kuran* (spirit) of Wambina, the mythical man who had created that part of the country. Moanya was most upset over the state of that sacred place. When all the stones were standing upright, Moanya explained, the aborigines in the country were feeling well; their legs were so strong they could walk long distances, and their arms so supple that their spears never missed their mark. Both men and women left the camp early in the morning to hunt for game and collect the grass seeds. Everyone was happy and full of energy.

But when the stones were lying down, as they were when we passed, the aborigines were always sleeping. They hung round the missions and the cattle stations for food; and the men did not hunt because their legs became tired, nor did the women labour hard to collect the grass seeds for the cakes. Until white men came into that country, the stones were always looked after. 'But,' said Moanya sadly, 'nobody cares now; the white man with his flour is killing us.'

It was difficult to get into Ungata water-hole. I was surprised that the camels were able to find a place for their feet among the tumbled boulders. But, in spite of a great deal of fuss and noise, they kept going until we reached a level spot where they could be unloaded. Without waiting, everyone went across to have a look at the water-hole, only to find that it was bone-dry. Moanya was the most surprised, for, he insisted, he had never seen it empty. However, he was still confident that the rock-hole on the top of the valley was permanent. So we sent Moanya and Jabiaba with buckets to bring some water back to camp; but long before we had prepared the evening meal, two very crestfallen aborigines returned with empty buckets, and shamefacedly announced, 'Kapi wia' (water none).

Although Ungata was a failure, and put us a day behind in our water supplies, the visit was well worth while. It was there, for the first time, that we were able fully to appreciate the strong link between the aboriginal myths and the country to which they belong, for every prominent feature in the landscape, even the large boulders and trees, were associated in some way or another with the exploits of the giant ancestors of the long-distant past. Moanya was so proud of Ungata that he begged us to stay the following day in order that he could tell us all about the place. But the thought that Piltadi might be dry, and of the frantic rush across the waterless desert to reach Oparinna before the camels collapsed from thirst, effectively prevented any loitering.

When I was writing my journal, just before going to bed, there was a brilliant flash of lightning, and a few drops of rain fell on the pages of my book. Quickly I woke Tjundaga and Lauri, and helped them pull the tarpaulin over the camel saddles and the perishables, then turned in, hoping the lightning was the prelude to a thunderstorm. Even a few points of rain at Ungata would have saved us, because the run-off from the floor of the gorge, a flat sheet of rock a quarter of a mile long and fifty yards wide, would have put more than sufficient water into the rock-hole to satisfy the camels and fill the canteens. But the storm passed over, with much noise and a few scattered drops. Hoping against hope that the storm would develop into a shower, I crept into my sleeping-bag and finally went to sleep from sheer weariness.

THE LETHAL STONE OF ULTURNA
"The stone is full of the kuranita of dysentery, and to touch it means death." *(Page 144.)*

THE LEGEND OF KUTUNGA AND THE WILD TOMATOES
"Both the tomatoes and the cakes, some of the latter badly cracked in drying,
are now . . . curiously shaped boulders on the hillside." *(Page 144.)*

Chapter XVIII

Piltadi and the Rainbow-serpent

THE FATES WERE ON OUR SIDE, for Piltadi still held two to three hundred gallons of black, putrid water, more than sufficient to give the camels a drink, while Moanya uncovered a soak, not known to the aboriginal girls, from which we were able to replenish the canteens. So for the time being our troubles about water were over.

Piltadi is at the end of a long, narrow gorge, with steep, rocky sides, covered with large boulders, spinifex and desert trees; and a level floor, whose surface is broken occasionally by conical piles of rocks. In normal seasons, Piltadi is a series of large rock-holes, but at the time of our visit only the top one held water. That curious hole, about ten feet long and three wide, had sides so steep and smooth that anyone who had fallen in would have been unable to climb out without help.

The camels, of course, could not drink from such a water-hole, so that every drop had to be carried down in buckets, and poured into a tarpaulin stretched over a bowl-shaped depression. I counted those buckets, and was surprised to find out that the five camels between them drank one hundred and twenty gallons; that is, each beast had inside of it twenty-four gallons, two hundred and forty pounds of water! Yet there was no difference in their appearance. I was amazed at the amount of water those animals stored away, and had often wondered if I had miscounted the buckets, until on re-reading Finlayson's *The Red Centre* I found that one of his camels, after three and a half days' dry stage, drank forty-three gallons!

During our stay at Piltadi we learned from Moanya the story of its creation. Away back in the time when the world was young, two Snake brothers and their wives lived near Piltadi. Every day the women went out hunting, and every

133

evening brought the game to the men, who seldom did anything but perform ceremonies. After a while, becoming
annoyed at the men's laziness, the women decided they
would eat all the food they caught, and leave the men to
look after themselves. The Snake-men were so angry, that
they made up their minds to punish the women for their
insubordination. Many schemes were suggested, and much
talking was done before the brothers agreed each to change
himself into a Wonambi (a giant mythical water serpent,
which also had the power to travel both above and below
ground at will) and play a practical joke upon the women
that would cause them a great deal of hard, useless labour.

Going to a marsupial rat hole, where the women had
been digging, the brothers first imitated the tracks of a large
snake by rubbing the back of a spear-thrower on the ground.
Then they entered the hole, one of them, however, leaving
out enough of his tail to attract the attention of the women.

Later, the younger sister, seeing the tracks of so large a
snake, and then its tail, became most excited, but when she
started to pull the creature from its burrow, its tail kept
slipping from her grasp. Actually the Wonambi, to tease
the woman, allowed himself to be dragged out for a few
feet before he wriggled himself free. Again and again he
let himself be caught, only to escape once more, until the
woman, becoming tired, gave up and returned to her sister.

While having their evening meal the younger sister said
to the elder:

'Today I almost caught a carpet snake as big as a
Wonambi, but I couldn't pull it from its burrow, it was too
strong for me.'

'I'll give you help to-morrow,' said the elder sister, 'and
we'll catch it, however big it is.'

The next morning the women set off, digging-sticks in
their hands, and wooden dishes on their heads. When they
reached the burrow of the marsupial rat, they saw fresh
tracks round its entrance (made by the Snake brothers). But
though the women dug all day long, at times seeing their
prey, they finished at sunset, hot and tired, without any

results for their strenuous work. All the next day the sisters laboured, and though again their quarry was often in sight, they caught only one small carpet snake, which they cooked and ate for their evening meal. And so the women dug on, following the Wonambi which continued to push their way through the ground, just out of reach. Occasionally the Snake brothers released one of their *kuran* as a small snake, thus giving the women sufficient food to keep them digging.

In their pursuit of that snake the two sisters dug a trench from Atjaratjara to Piltadi, now a water-course, some twenty miles long, visible evidence of those women's herculean labours. Then the burrow started to go deeper, and the work became more arduous. The sisters followed many side branches of the main burrow, only to find them either empty or occupied by a small snake. And that was how the women made the present gorge of Piltadi, with its many subsidiary creeks, and its conical piles of rock that clutter the valley floor.

At last, the elder sister changed her tactics, and dug a pit (now the largest rock-hole at Piltadi) ahead of the entrance to the burrow, and uncovered one of the Wonambi before he could get out of the way. His huge coils, turning round in the hole beneath the woman's feet, so alarmed her that she threw her digging-stick, and pierced the side of the creature. The other Wonambi left the burrow, chased and swallowed the younger woman, whilst the injured snake, although suffering great pain, caught, killed and ate the elder sister at the mouth of the present gorge.

That Wonambi is now a curiously-shaped bloodwood tree, with a dry limb standing out on one side, and the trunk covered with lumps and excrescences. The dead limb is the digging-stick, with which the snake was speared, the lumps and excrescences on the trunk the body of the woman still showing through the skin of the snake.

The legend of the Wonambi, known to the scientific world as the rainbow-serpent, belongs in one form or another to all living Australian tribes, and there is little doubt that the bunyip, which exercised the attention and the imagination of

our early settlers, was the same legendary creature. Many
scientists have added to our knowledge of the rainbow-
serpent, and I have traced it personally, in its various
manifestations, from the north coast of Australia, through
the central regions to the River Murray, and from Central
Australia well toward the western edge of the continent.

The serpent myth in the various Australian tribes has
many features in common. The snake is a huge creature,
many-coloured, with a mane, and often a beard; it is
feared by the aborigines because it attacks all strangers who
approach the water in which it lives, usually calling with a
deep, booming note. The rainbow-serpent is essentially the
water element in nature, and is related to everything that
the aborigines associate with water, rainbows, pearl-shells,
rivers, permanent springs and rock-holes. The serpent, being
afraid of the opposing natural element, fire, will always
endeavour to escape its influence. Even a small fire, such as
Matinya lit on the edge of the serpent-inhabited water-hole
on the summit of Ayers Rock, is sufficient to frighten the
creature to its underground home.

The curious aboriginal beliefs, linking fire, water, the
rainbow, and the Wonambi, are well illustrated in a legend
told to me by old Tjalerina.

One day, when two Rat-men were out hunting, they came
across what they thought was a carpet snake, but what was,
in reality, a young Wonambi, which had left its home in
a nearby water to look for food. The men captured the
serpent, and prepared to cook it. First they made a fire of
mulga, but as soon as they threw the Wonambi on the coals,
the *kuranita* or water essence in its body put out the fire.
Thinking something was wrong, the men collected a large
heap of the desert oak, which always makes a hot bed of
coals, but again the same thing happened. Entirely puzzled,
the men used the best wood they knew, that of the ironwood
tree, but although the heat was so great that the hunters
could hardly get near the fire, the moment the snake fell on
the glowing coals, they all went black. The men tried many
woods, bloodwood, corkwood, and various acacias, but with

no better results. Finally, as a last resort, they used samphire wood, a shrub whose leaves are soft, fleshy and particularly full of water. That fire kept its heat, the food was cooked, and the men had their fill.

But the snake was far too large for one meal, so, shouldering the remainder, the hunters set out for camp. Before many miles had passed they noticed that their legs were becoming stiff and painful, and by the time the camp was within sight, their limbs were so rigid that they could barely walk. On all sides of them were little snakes, some of the *kuran* of the Wonambi, each surrounded by a prismatic halo. The aborigines, unaware of the cause of their illness, were just able to struggle into camp before they became unconscious.

By the time the medicine men had been summoned, the hunters were as stiff and rigid as dead men. When the doctors saw the meat that had been brought in, and the small snakes everywhere, they knew at once the cause of the trouble. They killed the young snakes, burnt the remainder of the Wonambi (with samphire wood), and then attended to their patients. On opening the bodies the medicine men found the hunters were full of water and the algae that grows on stagnant pools, which the sick men had absorbed from the flesh of the Wonambi. The doctors cleaned out the algae, magically healed the openings, then placed the hunters between two large fires to drive the water (perspiration) from their bodies. The patients became conscious, their limbs relaxed, and in a short time they were walking about the camp, sadder, but wiser men.

Nothing shows more clearly than the legend of the rainbow-serpent that the aboriginal people of Australia were never entirely dissociated from world thought. The cult of the serpent, either as a real creature, a mythical being, or associated with a deity, was common throughout the ancient world, and still is among the primitive races of today. Even in the more specific form of a serpent, wearing a head-dress, it belongs both to ancient and modern times. Carvings on Celtic and Romo-Gallic altars depict horned serpents;

there are numerous representations of feathered serpents in ancient Chinese and Cambodian art; while Quetzal-coatl, the feathered serpent god of the extinct Central American, civilizations, belongs to rain and water. Coming forward into the present day, there is a still wider distribution of the mythical snake-like creature with a head ornament, which is associated with water, and sometimes with the rainbow. It is found among the Indians of Alaska and south-western United States, especially in the tribes of Arizona and New Mexico; it is also found in Western Africa, particularly in the tribes of primitive Bushmen, where a large horned serpent, similar to the Wonambi of the Central Australian desert, guards their water-hole. The Oriental dragon, with its highly symbolized head-dress, and Naga, the feathered serpent of the more southern parts of China, are also connected with rain and water.

Before we left Ernabella for Ayers Rock, Lauri and I had been made members of the tribe; Lauri was the tribal son to Moanya, while I was Numidi's brother. After Moanya had finished his story about the Snake-men, now living in the Piltadi rock-hole, Lauri told Moanya how much we admired his tribal country, particularly Piltadi gorge. The native man, gratified with our praise, replied impulsively:

'S'pose you bin sit down (camp) here for long time, Lauri, me give Piltadi to you; this one place your country. Numidi (his wife) and me bin camp alonga Ungata.'

Lauri was surprised and flattered at Moanya's offer. To be given a share in the lands of an aboriginal tribe, especially a place as attractive as Piltadi, is an experience which comes to few. I felt that Lauri had all the luck, for Numidi's country, with which I was associated, was in the desert, far south of the Mann Ranges. It was unlikely that I, like Lauri, would ever be able to look around me and think, 'This is my own, my native land.'

Lauri, now belonging to Piltadi, and related to the aborigines who owned it, was in no more danger of being attacked by the Wonambi that lived in the rock-hole than

Moanya himself. With me it was different. I was a stranger, and the mythical serpent always attacks strangers, so, for my own safety, I was not allowed to go near the rock-hole until Moanya could come and explain about me to the Wonambi. Later, with Lauri, Tjundaga, Jabiaba and Moanya, I stood on the edge of Piltadi, and looked down on that black, putrid water, while Moanya introduced me in this manner to the great, many-coloured serpent beneath its surface.

'This one, Miti Momforda, him *kurta* (elder brother) longa Numidi. Him close-up blackfella, you no more bin hurt him.'

Life has led me into strange places, and into stranger experiences, but surely my introduction to that Wonambi was the strangest of them all. So I was not far behind Lauri. He had Piltadi, but I, at least, had met the Wonambi.[1]

It rained at Piltadi on the second night of our stay; really, a series of spectacular thunderstorms, whose sound reverberated up and down the narrow gorge. Not a great deal of rain fell, but sufficient, as it turned out, to fill some of the rock-holes ahead of us. That rain lifted a big load from my mind. The Mann Ranges were one of the last places in Australia where the association between the aborigines, their lands, and their legendary stories was still complete. Already, as Moanya had said at Ungata, while he sorrowfully erected the fallen stones, 'The white man, with his flour, is killing us.' And in all too short a time, the opportunity of research on those aspects of their life will have passed away for ever. Not that we could do any more, in the time available, than gather a skeleton of the legends. Nevertheless that knowledge, inadequate as it is, should help to reveal the vital link between the aborigines and the land in which they live, and so, perhaps, lead to a deeper appreciation of his problems under the impact of our civilization.

[1] That experience was not unique. Spencer and Gillen, whose research on aboriginal life is an important part of Australian ethnology, were taken by their aboriginal companions to the home of the great Wollunqua snake of the Warramunga tribe, and introduced.

The old rain-maker, Tilbukuna, arrived just in time to see the success of his efforts. He was overjoyed, although he explained that the rain should have fallen two nights earlier (when we were at Ungata). But when it did not come, he and his companions made more *inma* (ceremony) and, lo and behold, there was the rain!

In spite of the fact that Tilbukuna had succeeded in making rain (I have seen other examples of native magic that worked), I still do not think that the aborigines, by means of sympathetic magic, expressed through a primitive ceremony, are able to control the complicated forces of nature that produce rain. Nevertheless, several irrefutable facts remain. Tilbukuna had no choice of time, he knew only a day beforehand that we were facing a dangerous water shortage; the rain fell in early September, quite out of season, the normal times being between November and March; it fell within the estimated period of five days; and—*it did rain.*

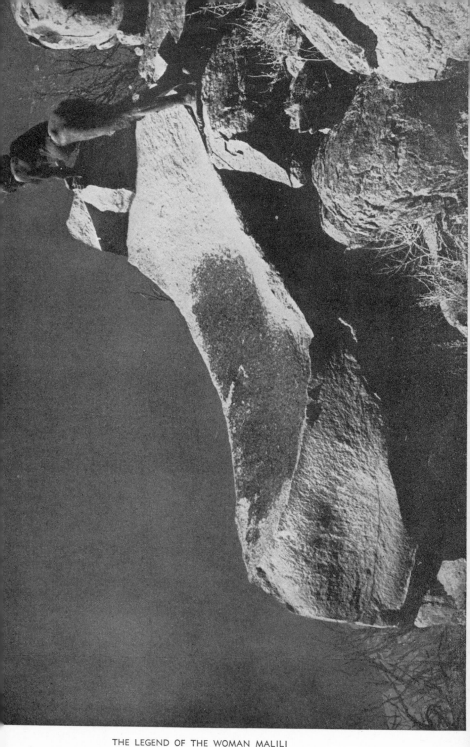

THE LEGEND OF THE WOMAN MALILI
"Her carrying dish a hollow boulder on the hillside." *(Page 145.)*

THE WATTLE-GUM INCREASE CEREMONY OF UNWARA
"Jabiaba . . . rubbed one of the boulders . . . while the other aborigines chanted
'Utunda, Utunda. Natunda, Natunda. Iriwa." *(Page 145.)*

CHAPTER XIX

The Legends of the Mann Ranges

THE FIRST SOUNDS WE HEARD each morning were the breaking of sticks, the crackling of flames, and the low voices of our brown-skinned companions, as they stirred our dormant camp-fire into life. The task was a voluntary one, done from a natural courtesy and a desire to help, and continued throughout the whole of our stay. Whether we were in the desert or the hills, whether the day was wet or fine, the same friendly sounds always awakened us. Usually there were sufficient coals left to start a blaze, but if not, one of the men would bring a stick from his own camp, for, as the aborigines have no other means of warming themselves, their fires are always kept burning.

The dry weather camps of the aboriginal people are very simple. Each one consists of a crescent-shaped windbreak of boughs about a foot high, shallow depressions in the sandy soil in which the occupants sleep, and fires, little larger than a dinner plate, one on either side of each sleeper. Ethnologists are puzzled as to how, under such primitive conditions, the naked aborigines can keep warm enough to sleep, especially as the temperature is often many degrees below freezing. It is possible that the native possesses some physical mechanism to meet those conditions, though on still evenings, when incidentally the nights are coldest, the heat rising from their tiny fires would cover their camps like a blanket, and keep the sleepers warm. But on nights such as the last evening at Piltadi, when a cold wind raged up and down the narrow gorge, the aborigines must suffer considerably, for the heat radiating from their fires would be quickly dissipated.

That cold, bleak weather continued all the next day. The blustering wind and light showers that tore across the plain and rough hills took the heart out of everyone. Even

Moanya, normally a good-tempered fellow, irritably told Tilbukuna, the rain-maker, that the second rain-making ceremony he had performed was the cause of the trouble; the first one at Oparinna would have brought all the rain that was wanted.

Tilbukuna, who was feeling as sorry for himself as was Moanya, agreed that he had made too much *inma* (ceremony), but explained that he had been anxious to show Tjamu (myself) that he really could make rain.

Lauri, Tjundaga and I tramped behind the camels to get some warmth in our nearly frozen bodies, and the aborigines carried burning sticks the size of small camp-fires. The fire-stick is a primitive, and, I had thought, an inefficient means of heating, until, on the advice of Jabiaba, I carried one myself. I was then surprised at the amount of comfort that could be gained from so simple a device, for the heat from the fire-stick kept my hands as well as my face and body warm. Also, I was surprised at the care and skill required to keep the stick alight. Until Jabiaba had taught me how to hold it, the direction the wind should blow on it, and the way to keep it burning freely by swinging it across my body, the fire-stick either went out or scorched my fingers. In fact, I called so often on Jabiaba for assistance that finally he lost patience.

'P'raps you cleva fella 'longa white man's things, Tjamu,' said the kindly old man, 'but you bin know nodin 'bout *waru* (fire).'

Among the aborigines that was true. Making fire is to them as natural as breathing; even the smallest children are expert in its use.

For the next few days we travelled along the southern edge of the Mann Ranges. To most white men that country is desolate, unfriendly, 'the land that God forgot.' The aboriginal's outlook is the reverse. To him the landscape abounds with interest. The trees are not just trees, but the transformed bodies of bygone heroes; creeks are not just places where the water runs, but the tracks of gigantic serpents that meandered their way across the country; and isolated hills, not just piles of rocks, but ancestral camps, or heaps of discarded food, or, as in Piltadi, piles of earth thrown out by the women in their long task. We passed the works of many creators in those days, those of the Sleepy Lizard, the Mountain-devil, the Bell-bird, and Kundala with his dogs.

Probably the most interesting spots we visited were Kanbi, where the Emu and Wild Turkey quarrelled over their chicks; Ulturna, where Kutunga, the mother of the spirit children of the tribe, made cakes from wild tomatoes; Purtunya, where there is a stone, once the body of an initiate, the mere touch of which means death; and Unwara, where the woman, Malili, collected many foods before she was killed.

Gathering the details of those myths was not without its difficulties. Tjundaga, as the interpreter, would ask my question in the native tongue, and repeat the answer to me in English. The procedure sounds simple, but in practice was often the reverse. The men were so keen to tell me their stories that sometimes two or three would answer together, each giving a different aspect of the same legend, and so confusing the poor interpreter that he did not know what to tell me. Tjundaga would repeat the question, and would be about to pass on the correct answer, when, as often as not, one of the men would remember a song belonging to the myth, which would start them all chanting at the top of their voices. We would wait for the exuberance of the men to die down, then patiently find out the main thread of the story, and then the topographical details to which it was related.

The legend of the Emu,[1] Tjakara, and the Wild Turkey,[2] Kipara, widespread in aboriginal mythology, explains why the emu of the present day has many chicks, and the wild turkey but few. Although the legend has variants, the general story tells of a time when the two birds, each of which had large families, lived in the same camp. The Emu, however, was a jealous person, who wanted to be

[1] *Dromaius novae-hollandiae.*   [2] *Eupodotis australus.*

more important than her companion. So one day, returning from the hunt with only two chicks, she told the Wild Turkey that she had killed the remainder of her family, because they were too much trouble. After some persuasion, the Wild Turkey agreed to follow the example of her companion; but no sooner had she done so, than the Emu displayed the whole of her brood, and mocked the then distressed mother for her foolishness. The revenge of the Wild Turkey usually ends in the Emu being deprived of the power of air-borne flight, and condemned to roam the earth at the mercy of the dogs and men.

Ulturna, in one of the valleys west of Kanbi, was another interesting place. There, Kutunga, a woman of *tjukurita* (Creation Times) collected many wild tomatoes, and made them into cakes, which she placed in the sun to dry. Both the tomatoes and the cakes, some of the latter badly cracked in drying, are now to be seen as curiously shaped boulders on the hillside.

Only a short distance from where Kutunga had made the cakes is a curious, clinker-like rock, just showing above the ground. That rock was once a part of the body of Tapinya, a young initiate, who, when running along the face of a cliff to avoid being seen by the women, had fallen and was killed. The aborigines believe that the stone is full of the *kuranita* of dysentery, and that to touch it means death. Even to break a twig from a nearby tree, or to dig in the ground within a quarter of a mile of that stone, is to expose oneself to considerable danger. The aborigines keep the stone covered with branches and leaves, for they believe that, if it were to melt in the hot weather, all the people in the world would suffer from dysentery.

The woman Malili had lived at Unwara, one of the deep bays on the southern edge of the Mann Ranges. In the middle of that bay is a picturesque group of red boulders, decorated with native pines, and surrounded by a sea of silver grass. Viewed in the early morning light, that scene had all the delicate beauty of an old Chinese print, and I was not surprised to learn that it was linked with the

"As each man told us the history of a kulpidji (ceremonial object) he pressed his face and body against it, because . . . the kulpidji, being full of the kuranita of good health, made him feel well." *(Page 146.)*

". . . big patches of mulga (Acacia aneura) . . . are most uninteresting. In isolation, however, many of the trees are beautiful to look upon." *(Page 148.)*

mythology of the aborigines, for in no other aspect of their
culture is the sense of the beautiful, or the dramatic, better
shown than in the choice of their legendary places.

Those boulders at Unwara are the metamorphosed pieces
of wattle-gum left behind, in 'Creation Times,' by Malili,
and are consequently full of the *kuranita* or life-essence of
wattle-gum. Those boulders are now an 'increase centre,'
where rituals are performed to make the various acacia trees
exude their gum more freely.

The increase ceremony that the men staged at Unwara
was typical of many. Jabiaba, who was in charge, rubbed
one of the boulders with an upper grinding stone, whilst
the other aborigines chanted,

    'Utunda, utunda, natunda, natunda, iriwa,'
a chant that told the *kuranita* of the wattle-gum to 'Go to
the ironwood tree; go to the mulga tree; go to the witcheddy
bush,' and to every other gum-bearing tree. The dust made
by the rubbing, being the life-essence of the gum, 'flew' into
the air, and, under the influence of the rituals, 'stuck' to the
specific tree, and started to grow into nodules of gum.

Although the ceremonials for the increase of many of the
living creatures are more complex, the same fundamental
idea holds good. The finely powdered fragments of the
ancestral body, made potent by the chants, flies into the
air, and impregnates the particular creatures. The increase
centres are scattered all over the country, some in the terri-
tory of one family, some in that of another. Each family
group, at the proper time and place, must perform the
rituals associated with their own land, so that 'everyone in
the world,' to use an aboriginal term, will have sufficient
food. Therefore, if the natives want rain, or are without
kangaroos, grass seeds, wattle-gum, or other necessities, they
produce them by the appropriate ritual; for the aboriginal
is, or thinks he is, in charge of his own environment, and
does not propitiate a Supreme Being in order to gain favours.

The woman Malili is associated with three remarkable
rock formations at Unwara; the wattle-gum, which she left
behind, now an increase centre; her carrying dish, a hollow

L

boulder on the hillside; and herself, a group of rocks that resemble a human body. Malili met her death at the hands of the giant Pungalunga-men from Katatjuta (Mt. Olga), because she rested too near the cave in which they had hidden their ceremonial objects, the *kulpidji*.

Lauri and I had been shown the *kulpidji* belonging to that place. We were not allowed to approach the cave on the hillside in which they were stored, but had to sit on some rocks until the men brought down the sacred objects and laid them before us. As each man told us the history of a *kulpidji*, he pressed his body and face against it, because, he explained, the *kulpidji*, being full of the *kuranita* of good health, made him feel well.

The *kulpidji* are thin, narrow slabs of wood, about six feet in length, engraved with curious concentric-square designs. Some of them must be of great age, for their engravings have been almost worn away by the rubbing of fat and red ochre on their surfaces.

The *kulpidji* of the Pitjendadjara tribe are similar to the well-known *tjurunga* or *churinga* of the Aranda tribe of the Macdonnell Ranges in Central Australia. Among the Aranda the *tjurunga*, supposedly made by the mythical ancestors of the past, are the central part of their philosophical life, and the stories associated with them all belong to the Creation period. Before the advent of white man, many thousands of those *tjurunga* were stored in the caves and other hiding places throughout the Aranda country, and on the surface of each one was engraved, in particularly primitive symbolism, the Creation story of the locality with which it was associated.

Although the *kulpidji* of the Pitjendadjara are so sacred that no woman or uninitiated youth is allowed to look upon them, they are not as important in the philosophy of the tribe as the *tjurunga* are to the Aranda people. The men were unable to give a coherent account of either the engraved designs or the mythological stories associated with any of the *kulpidji* at Kanbi. All of them, purchased from adjacent tribes, had cost many spears and spear-throwers.

Not far from where Lauri and I had seen the *kulpidji* was the grave of a member of an early exploring party, who had been killed by one of his companions. The sight of that grave started the aborigines talking about the early days of the invasion of the white man, and the stories their fathers had told them about those times.

When the first Europeans, with their camels, came into the desert country, the aborigines were curious, but not belligerent. But when the white men started to shoot the native people, they were not only terrified at such brutality, but were totally at a loss to explain the killing, for they had no parallel behaviour in their own culture. Not knowing that the white man shot because he was afraid, or for the mere joy of taking life, the aborigines, after much discussion, came to the conclusion that the camels were huge dogs, and that their companions had been killed to provide those creatures with meat. When a native was killed, the aboriginal law of vengeance, or reciprocal killing, came into action, and attempts were made to spear the intruders. But the natives with their primitive weapons had no chance against the white men with their rifles, and so still more native people met their death.

The aborigines told us many stories of killings in the past, and even at the present time. They were still resentful over a cold-blooded murder of some of their companions which had occurred less than four years before our visit among them. A white dogger, trespassing on the aboriginal reserve, had, because of an argument over women, left poisoned flour, treacle and sugar behind in his camp. Four innocent men and two boys died before the aborigines realized that the food was poisoned.

Chapter XX

The Legend of Nintaka, the Lizard

WITHIN A FEW DAYS OF leaving Piltadi we were again in trouble about water. The rain had been patchy, and, although we were able to replenish the canteens from an occasional catchment, we could not find one large enough to give the camels a drink. Several times we left the main route to visit rock-holes, which the aborigines said were reliable, only to find them absolutely dry. So we decided to try our luck at Mulara, a spring in the Tomkinson Ranges which lay to the south.

On leaving the foot-hills of the Mann Ranges and entering the desert country, I was surprised at the luxuriance of the flora. Evidently an isolated thunderstorm had passed that way some months previously, for acacia trees, hibiscus and purple parakeelya were blooming everywhere. The sandy slopes of one valley were dotted with hundreds of wild peach trees,[1] their branches bending under the weight of scarlet fruit. Those peaches were a Godsend! Our continuous diet of damper, not always well cooked, had played havoc with my digestion. I had been able to get through a few bad patches on tinned tomatoes, and later on dry breakfast cereals, but we had no more, and I was doing a quiet starve. A small meal of peaches made me feel better, in fact, that fruit tided me over my last and worst attack.

It took us three hours to pass through that verdant area of fresh, green plants, a welcome and pleasing change after the eternal mulga scrubs, for big patches of mulga, with its sparse, dark-green foliage, are most uninteresting. In isolation, however, many of the trees are beautiful to look upon, especially when the delicate tracery of their branches is backed by a cloud-flecked sky, or a desert sunset.

The first sight of Mulara gave us a shock, for we thought it was empty. But, after we had cleaned out a foot of sand, the water began to run in slowly, so slowly indeed that it took two whole days to satisfy the camels and fill the

[1] *Eucarya acuminata.*

canteens. Yet we left Mulara with the pleasant feeling that in that vast country there were two places at least on which we could depend, Mulara and Piltadi.

Returning by a different route, we reached the edge of the Mann Ranges near Lake Wilson. That dry lake made me realize how lucky were both Giles and Gosse when they explored that country, for Mt. Olga, Oparinna, and many other springs were then running streams, and Lake Wilson was full of water.

Giles, in *Australia Twice Traversed*, writes:

On our arrival at the Lake we found its waters slightly brackish; there was no timber on the shores; it lay close under the foot of the mountains, having their rocky shores for the northern bank. The opposite shores were sandy; numerous ducks and water-fowls were floating on its breast. Several springs from the ranges ran into its northern shore, and on its eastern edge a large creek ran in, though its timber did not grow all the way. The water is now eight or nine miles around; it was of an oblong form, whose greatest length was east and west. When quite full this place must be at least twenty miles in circumference; I name this fine sheet of water Lake Wilson.

As I stood on that barren shore, and watched the heated air rise in small whirlwinds from its arid, dusty surface, I found it hard to realize that, when the first white men explored the Mann Ranges, that dusty lake bed was a large sheet of water, fed by streams and dotted with wild fowl.

From Lake Wilson we moved to Arana, an important place in the long and complicated legend associated with Nintaka, the Lizard or Perentie-man.[1]

The legend relates how, in the long distant times, the women of the Mann Ranges had only rough grinding-stones and, in consequence, their grass-seed cakes were coarse and unpalatable. Their men searched far and wide for flatter and finer-textured stones, but without success. One day when Nintaka, the Perentie-man, was out hunting, he heard, a long way to the east, a woman grinding seed for the evening meal. Nintaka listened intently, for he realized the sound of that distant grinding could only be made by a

[1] *Varanus giganteae.*

stone which was fine and smooth. So he made up his mind to go to that country, steal the grinding-stone, and bring it back to his own people.

For many days Nintaka journeyed towards the sound, each day getting nearer and nearer, until it finally led him to the Ninjuri (Black Lizard) people, who had made their camp not far from where the town of Oodnadatta now stands. Nintaka did not go into the camp, but lit a fire within sight of it, a custom that was, and still is, demanded by aboriginal etiquette. When the Ninjuri-men went out to meet Nintaka, he, naturally, did not tell them the real object of his visit, but related a fictitious story of his wanderings and the direction from which he had come.

Although Nintaka was forbidden the main camp for several days, he shared in the food of the community. Every evening a woman brought him a meal of kangaroo meat, and grass-seed cakes made from the finest flour he had ever tasted.

'My word,' thought he, as he munched the tasty cakes, 'won't my people be pleased when they are able to have cakes as good as these.'

After several days of impatient waiting, Nintaka entered the camp of the Ninjuri, and saw, at last, the grinding-stone he had travelled so many miles to possess, a flat slab of fine-grained sandstone, worn smooth by constant rubbing. It was so superior to those used by his own tribe that he could hardly wait until the time was ripe for him to steal it.

That evening Nintaka cut his foot; not a big cut, but large enough to make the blood flow and give the appearance of a serious wound. When, next morning, the Ninjuri-men came to take him out hunting, Nintaka showed them the wound, bemoaning the fact that he could not join them. Not realizing the deceitfulness of their guest, the Ninjuri-men expressed regrets at his misfortune, and went their way.

As soon as Nintaka had the camp to himself, he stole the grinding-stone and the head-ring on which it was carried, and swallowed them for safe-keeping. Then, to confuse the Ninjuri-men, for he knew they would try to catch him,

Nintaka made footmarks in all directions, changed himself into a small lizard, stepped lightly on the stones so that his footprints could not be seen, and travelled until he was many miles distant. As a final precaution, he made a heavy rain with his *ringili* (pearl-shell) to blot out any tracks he might have left behind.

After that he changed himself back to his original form and set out on the long, five hundred miles journey to the Mann Ranges, for he was anxious to show the treasure to his own people.

The Ninjuri-men, angry over the loss of their precious grinding-stone, prepared to capture and kill the thief. But when the hunters tried to track Nintaka they became thoroughly confused, for, although his footmarks led in all directions, they always finished in the centre of the camp. The hunters travelled in wider and wider circles to 'cut' his tracks, but without success. They had almost given up hope, when one of their number, who had been on a visit to the west, came in with the news that he had seen where Nintaka had walked across a patch of wet ground. Full of new hope, the Ninjuri-men set out again.

Meanwhile Nintaka, the Perentie-man, having made his way through the Everard and Musgrave Ranges, had reached the northern side of the Mann Ranges, where he climbed to the crest of a low hill to see if his enemies were following. As there was no sign of them, he disgorged the ill-gotten grinding-stone and head-ring. At Wankaringa we saw a spectacular group of rocks which commemorates that incident; the upper is Nintaka, with his head raised, searching for enemies; the one immediately below, the stolen grinding-stone; and an egg-shaped boulder, lower down the hillside, the head-ring on which the stone was carried.

Nintaka, thinking he was safe, and hungry from his long journey, ate so many mistletoe berries that they gave him a severe stomach-ache. A bloodwood tree, with a large bole near the ground, is visible evidence of the pain the Perentie-man suffered because of his gluttony.

Further west, Nintaka, having collected grass seeds, stopped for the first time to try out his prize. He was so pleased with the excellence of the grinding-stone, that he ground more flour, and made a larger damper than he required. The excess flour was later transformed into high cliffs, and the damper into a large boulder at their base.

When Nintaka reached camp everyone sang his praises, not only for the long, arduous journey he had undertaken, but also for the fine grinding-stone he had brought back.

After some time, convinced that the ruse to obliterate his tracks had been successful, Nintaka left the grinding-stone near the Arana water-hole when he went out hunting. One day, however, as he was returning to the camp, he heard the sound of his enemies, the Ninjuri-men, tramping on the precious grinding-stone, and breaking it to pieces. He rushed to avenge its destruction, only to be met by a number of armed men. Seeing the hopelessness of the situation, he ran up the side of a hill to escape, but his enemies followed, fixed him with several spears and killed him.

We spent a long, hot afternoon climbing over the hills to see the legendary places associated with that last encounter: the broken grinding-stone, now piles of flat rocks at the Arana water-hole; where Nintaka climbed the hill to escape his enemies, a steep, narrow gorge; and the Ninjuri-men, twisted corkwood trees.

The body of the dead Perentie-man, Nintaka, is a curious geological feature, consisting of an almost circular column of rock, about forty feet in length and two in diameter, lying prone on the hillside. The column has a number of fissures at right angle to its length, which, Jabiaba told us, were the knife cuts made by the infuriated Ninjuri-men. The aborigines would not touch that stone, for they feared the spirit of Nintaka would come out and injure them. Tjundaga was severely reprimanded because he tried to pull a tuft of grass from its base, and even Tilbukuna, the rain-maker, when I asked him to pose for a photograph, would not sit too close.

The aborigines, having completed the legend of Nintaka and the Ninjuri-men, led us to the Arana spring, which seeps from a hole in the base of a high cliff. I was puzzled how they were going to get a drink from that spring, for the reservoir was a good eighteen inches from the mouth of the opening, the aperture so small that it would only admit a medium-sized dog, and the aborigines had no water vessel. Again I saw their ingenuity at work. Moanya collected a handful of mulga grass, and, after breaking and twisting the grass somewhat, made it into a pad. Reaching into the spring, he held the pad in the water until it was saturated, then, taking it out, sucked it dry. Even though the day was hot, and Moanya had been without water for several hours, he was able to satisfy his thirst in about two minutes. Tjundaga and two other aborigines followed suit, using the same pad, and three dogs crawled in and drank their fill. Tjundaga then passed me a dirty tin, in which he kept his native tobacco, assuring me that, by then, the water in the spring was quite clean.

Clean, ye gods! I wondered what were his ideas of cleanliness. Four men had soaked the same grass pad in that tiny water, and three dogs had had a drink. After that, with a foul tobacco tin as a cup, it was my turn! I almost refused, but my tongue was as dry as a board, and the canteens were two miles away over the rough hills. So, dogs and all, I drank; not much, just sufficient to wet my mouth. Lauri was more venturesome; possibly he did not realize the danger, for many a white man has had years of illness through drinking unboiled water from such springs. Fortunately neither of us suffered any after-effects, though it might easily have been otherwise.

That evening it rained heavily. Tilbukuna's rain-making certainly had been successful! The downpour having filled the nearby rock-holes, we felt there should be no further trouble about water, though we knew if the waters on the northern side of the Mann Ranges were dry we might have to re-visit Piltadi.

About three o'clock in the morning the sky became clear and the stars, shining through the rain-washed air, extraordinarily brilliant. The beauty of the firmament has always fascinated me; many times from the warmth of my sleeping-bag I have watched the worlds above me, those glistening pin-points of light that seemed to hang just over my head.

Although in the early days among the aborigines my wonder, as well as my admiration, of the stars had been great, they were backed by little information. True, I could recognize Orion, Scorpio and, of course, the Southern Cross; but the constellations of Argo, Delphinus, Hercules and many others were beyond me. But when the native men started to tell me their stories of the night sky, it became necessary for me to improve my astronomical knowledge so that I could recognize the aboriginal constellations. Since then I have gathered legends of their star-lore concerning all parts of the sky; the Milky Way, the Southern Cross, Argo, and Venus and Jupiter, known as the hunter and his dog, sometimes the one in front, sometimes the other. Even now I cannot exhaust their fund of sky myths. Perhaps one of these days an ethno-astronomer will visit my brown-skinned companions, and record all their celestial legends.

I know of only one aboriginal love story, such as fills our literature to repletion, and that is associated with a group of stars in the tail of Scorpio. It relates how there once lived a young boy and girl who were very much attached to each other. When the lad was almost fully grown, he was taken from the camp, and the companionship of the girl, to undergo the rites of initiation, which occupy a year or more. That separation distressed the girl, especially as the time for the initiation drew near, for she knew, in a vague way, about the painful ordeals through which her lover would have to pass. So at the initiation, when the women were told to leave, the girl broke the strictest of all aboriginal laws and, under the cover of darkness, stayed behind to watch the ceremony she was forbidden to see. When it was over, an old man took the initiate to a separate camp, where, tired out with the long rituals, he soon fell asleep. But the youth

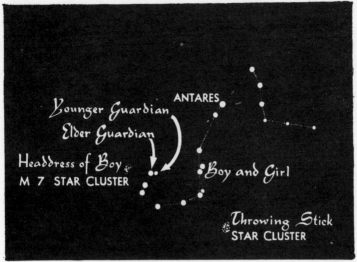

. . . Only one aboriginal love story . . . associated with the tail of Scorpio. (Page 154.)

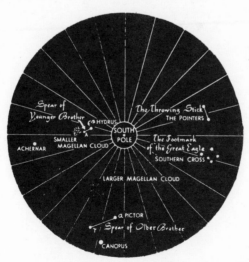

Another sky legend is associated with the Magellanic Clouds. (Page 156).

himself could not rest, because of the pain of his newly
inflicted wound.

The girl, distraught over the suffering of the youth, and
the thought of their long separation, decided to take him
from the old man, and travel to some distant country where
they could live together in peace. Worming her way close
to the camp, she attracted the boy's attention by making the
low cry of an animal, then, with signs, persuaded him to
come to her. But no sooner were the young couple together
than the guardian woke to replenish his fire. Knowing that
death awaited them, for both had committed unpardonable
offences, the girl put her arms round the boy, and 'flew' with
him into the sky.

When he realized his charge was gone, the guardian called
his younger brother, and together they searched the ground
for tracks, which soon told them what had happened. Looking upward, they saw the fugitives travelling rapidly along
the Milky Way. The brothers attempted to climb into the
sky in pursuit of the escaping lovers, but their feet kept
slipping and thus created many of the stars in that part
of the firmament. Finally they succeeded and strode along
the Milky Way with great steps (paired stars are now their
footmarks). A boomerang, thrown by the younger brother,
just missed the girl, but the throwing-stick of the elder
struck the boy's head with such a blow that it knocked off
his *pukati* (head-dress). Now they are all turned to stars,
and shine in the tail of Scorpio, the two guardians, the
initiate, and the foolish but faithful girl.

Another sky story that has a wide circulation refers to the
constellations of Orion and the Pleiades (the Seven Sisters).
Many races have stories about the Pleiades, and the majority,
like our own, refer to them as 'the women.' Orion, on the
other hand, is generally a man, and not always a desirable
fellow.

To the aborigines of the desert, Orion is the ancestor,
Nirunya, who was forever chasing the Pleiades, the Kunkarunkara women. Again and again the women came to
earth to escape his unwelcome attentions, but always they

were discovered and had to flee. Usually the Kunkarunkara women were too clever for Nirunya, and he was outwitted, but now and again one of the women fell victim to his desires.

Many of the natural features of Central Australia were created during the various encounters between Nirunya and the Kunkarunkara women. At one place they came together to gather food.

'Here they made their camp,' Numidi told me in her native tongue, pointing to hollows in the rock where two of the star-women had slept, 'and early next morning they started to dig for tubers. But Nirunya (the man of Orion) had seen them from his sky home, and, waiting until they were engrossed in their task, endeavoured to capture them. Seeing him coming, the women went underground for a short distance, then burst out and escaped to the sky.'

The marks of that encounter are there today: the sleeping place, the pit from which they emerged, and, on a flat rock-surface, a hole dug by one of them in her search for food. Lying beside that hole is a block of stone, the transformed carrying-dish, which the woman left behind in her headlong flight.

Another sky legend associated with the Magellanic Clouds, Achernar and Canopus, is concerned with the fundamental belief in the reward for goodness, and the punishment of evil.

The Magellanic Clouds are the homes of two celestial beings, the Kungara, the larger cloud belonging to the elder, the smaller to the younger brother. When an aboriginal is dying, the young brother takes his death-dealing spear and goes to earth to capture the *kuran* (spirit) of the dead man. If the dying man has led a good life, the elder Kungara, who is a much kindlier fellow, will prevent his brother from capturing the spirit. On the other hand, if the dying man has led an evil life, the older Kungara does not interfere, but allows his brother to spear the *kuran* of the dead man, take it to Achernar (the younger Kungara's camp-fire), cook and eat it.

While we were at Ernabella, Jabiaba had made a drawing of a constellation low down on the northern sky, which including all the stars of Delphinus, Lyra, Aquila, and parts of Cygnus and Hercules. It represented a family of Kanga (Crow people). Vega, in Lyra, is the mother crow watching her son (Altair in Aquila) showing off his new feather decorations, which he had placed at the tip of each wing (now the third magnitude star in the east, and the fourth magnitude star to the west of Altair). The father crow, seated by a water-hole with a number of pieces of meat he had cooked, forms the constellation of Delphinus; whilst the remaining stars of Aquila, Lyra, the arm of Hercules, and Albireo in Cygnus, are either the footprints of the family or pieces of their cooked meat.

Many and delightful are the stories about sky-people, the Milky Way, the Coal Sack, the Southern Cross, the Pointers, and the False Cross in Argo. Although some of the star-dwellers have lost their interest in the world below, there are others who can still wield a power, for good or ill, in the affairs of man.

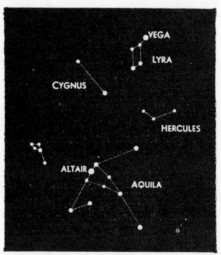

The legend of the Crow family. (P. 157)

CHAPTER XXI

The Spirit Children

EVER SINCE LEAVING ERNABELLA
Jabiaba had been anxious to take us to his birthplace, the
Niunya rock-holes. Knowing that the mythical woman,
Kutunga, the mother of the spirit children, also belonged
to that place, we were as anxious to go there as the old
man was to take us. On reaching Niunya we found that not
only the rock-holes, but all the surrounding country, was
linked with the legend of Kutunga and her unwanted lover,
Milbili, the Lizard-man.

Milbili had pursued Kutunga for some time. He finally
caught and raped her at the Niunya rock-holes, where,
before he took her away to the north-west, she gave birth
to quadruplets, two normal and two deformed infants.
Those infants are now boulders; two of them, egg-shaped,
contain an inexhaustible supply of healthy spirit children,
the little silvery-haired *yulanya*; the other boulders, similar
in shape, but more irregular in outline, are the source of all
the misshapen babies.

If more children are required by the group, the men,
strictly shunning the transformed bodies of the deformed
infants, go to the *yulanya* stones, and, while chanting a song,
place short green twigs between the boulders. The little
spirits, stimulated by the chants, leave their home, carrying
the *kuran* of a twig, not the twig itself, and visit the camps
of the aborigines, looking for desirable mothers. Having
made their choice, each *yulanya* waits until the woman is off
her guard, enters her body and begins life as a human being.
The little spirits are so small that they can only be seen by
the medicine-men, who, in fact, sometimes help the spirit
children to find mothers.[1]

[1] It is practically certain that there are child increase centres associated
with the other ancestral beings, although we did not gather information as
specific as that relating to the *yulanya* (child spirits) of Kutunga.

Tialerina holding a perentie (Varanus giganteus).   (Page 149.)

THE LEGEND OF THE PERENTIE-MAN, NINTAKA

"Nintaka . . . eat so many mistletoe berries that they gave him a severe stomach-ache. The blood-wood tree, with a large bole near the ground, is visible evidence of the pain." (Page 151.)

The day Jabiaba took us to see the *yulanya* stones, we asked him to show us how the little child spirits were coaxed from their homes. Although the old man did not refuse, he was very half-hearted about the matter, complaining, as he laid some green twigs between the two boulders,

'Too many *idi* (babies) 'bout camp already; man can't get no sleep night-time.'

The belief of the Pitjendadjara in the supernatural origin of their children tended to confirm the conclusions reached by other workers and myself, that the aborigines did not understand physical paternity; that is, they did not associate the father with the birth of the child. In fact, I have met aborigines who, even though they have been in contact with our civilization for three generations, still hold to their original beliefs.

Mulili, an old lady of the Flinders Range tribe, told me that their spirit children, the *muri*, came from two great mothers, the *maudlanami*, who lived above the blue vault of heaven. The *muri* flew down to the earth like tiny butter-flies, fed on the nectar of the gum-tree blossoms during the day, and slept under loose pieces of bark by night, until they found the mother they wanted.

When old Mulili had finished her explanation of human origins, I said to her:

'Well, that's the blackfellow's story of how you came into the world, but do you really think it is the right one? You know what the white-fellow says about it.'

'Yes,' agreed Mulili, 'I know what the white-fellow says, but I don't think he is right. If he is, then married women should be having babies all the time, for they're always living with their husbands.'

'But they don't,' she went on; 'some women have many children, some have few, and some have none at all. The white man can't explain that, but the blackfellow can. If one of our women has a lot of babies, we know she is a favourite of the *muri*, the little children from the sky; if another has only a few children, then only an odd *muri* wants her for a mother; and if a woman hasn't any, then

M1

everyone knows that the little spirit children don't like her, and won't use her body to become a human being.'

'No,' concluded the old lady, 'I don't think the white-fellow is right, because he can't explain those things, and we can.'

Old Mulili's argument, coupled with the teachings of the Pitjendadjara people about the spirit children in the *yulanya* stones, indicated that the aborigines were not aware of the true nature of conception and birth. Nevertheless, the incident in the legend of Kutunga and Milbili, where Kutunga had borne children after she had been raped, a direct connection between sexual intercourse and birth, made me wonder if the hypothesis was quite so watertight as I had first thought. It is possible that the aborigines are aware, to a limited degree, of the facts of procreation, but as they are at variance with the doctrines laid down in the legendary stories, the native people consider those physical facts as being relatively unimportant, and accept only their philo-sophical beliefs, as indeed we do in many phases of our own religious life.

Although there is little or no ceremony belonging to the birth of a child, there is always a good deal of interest in the event, especially among the women. While we were at Ernabella, Nibiana came across to our camp one morning bubbling over with excitement.

'Tell missus,' she said to me, '*idi* (baby) bin come 'long night-time. Him girl too.'

As she was the first girl born in the camp for some time, all the women were in quite a fluster about her. 'Johnnie' needed no second telling. Quickly she gathered a few dainties for the mother, and, accompanied by Nibiana, as well as all the other women in the camp, went along to see the new infant.

My wife found the mother lying down, surrounded by a low breakwind of boughs, and, between her back and a small fire, was the baby girl, less than ten hours old. The babe was remarkably light-skinned and, except for a slight duskiness across the buttocks and round the nipples, about

THE LEGEND OF THE PERENTIE-MAN, NINTAKA

"At Wankaringa we saw a spectacular group of rocks, . . . the upper was Nintaka with his head raised . . . ; the one immediately below, the stolen grinding stone; and an egg-shaped boulder . . . the head ring on which the ginding stone was carried." (Page 151.)

The LEGEND OF THE PERENTIE-MAN, NINTAKA

"The body of the dead Perentie-man consists of an almost circular column of rock, about forty feet in length, and two in diameter." *(Page 152.)*

the colour of a sunburnt European. However, her little body darkened quickly, and in about a week she was the same colour as her mother.

The native women stroked the baby with great affection, pointing out her virtues, the long hair, the well-formed body and tiny hands, clucking over the child as any group of white women would over one of their own kind.

We found out later that the mother was alone when the child was born. As the pains of birth had developed, the woman, aided by a young girl, arranged a windbreak some distance from the camp, and lit a fire. The young girl left the mother to attend to the duties of childbirth unaided. We were assured that that was the usual custom, especially if a woman has had a number of children. Contrary to the usual stories about aboriginal birth, the woman did not move from her camp until after the third day. No doubt, if the whole tribe had been on the move, she would have had to travel much sooner, but to do so would have meant a great deal of pain and discomfort.

Now that we had seen the actual place of the spirit children, and as both our time and food were running short, we turned for home.

The party had been without meat for some days, for we had seen little game, and that far beyond the range of a rifle. My companions had a most exaggerated idea of the killing power of the rifle. They seemed to think that so long as a kangaroo was in sight, I merely had to point the rifle in its direction, pull the trigger, and the days of the beast were numbered. Repeatedly, during those meatless days, I heard the aborigines excitedly call, "Kuka, kuka (meat, meat), Tjamu,' only to see, quite out of range, a kangaroo hopping away from us. Always the men wanted me to follow the creature, and always I refused; for I knew my limited abilities as a hunter and a rifle shot, and, besides, my last pair of canvas shoes had almost gone to pieces.

One cold morning, as I sat freezing on the camel, the keen eyes of the native men sighted four emus about a quarter of a mile distant. That time the conditions had possibilities,

for the emus were not alarmed, they were up-wind, and
there was sufficient ground cover to allow me to approach
more closely to the birds. Slipping quietly from the back
of the camel, I crept toward the emus, taking advantage of
every tree or shrub, until I reached the trunk of a desert
oak. From there about three hundred yards of open spinifex-
covered flat separated me from the birds. Although the emus
were feeding quietly, I knew that the moment I showed
myself they would be off, and our chance of a good meat
meal with them. So, setting the sights, I took very careful
aim, pulled, the trigger, and hoped for the best.

I saw one of the birds drop, and the others, unaware of
the direction from which the shot was fired, ran toward me,
one of the largest of them stopping within a hundred yards
of where I was crouched. Quickly slipping another cartridge
into the rifle, I fired, and missed. The bullet sailed harm-
lessly overhead, for in my excitement I had forgotten to
reset the sights. There were cries of disappointment from
behind, for neither Lauri, Tjundaga, nor the aborigines had
seen the first emu fall. But their cries were quickly changed
when I signalled the success of the first shot. The men, led
by old Jabiaba, ran forward and danced around me, calling
out extravagant words of praise as they made playful jabs
at my legs with their spears. Really, I felt quite a hero.

As a matter of fact I was as pleased as they were, and a
great deal more surprised, but, being the hunter, I tried to
appear indifferent, just as if I could shoot an emu any day,
and at any time. Actually the shot was the merest fluke.
With a heavy cross-wind blowing, I had hit that emu in the
neck, at a range of three hundred yards. A most unfortunate
bird! When Tjundaga complimented me on my marksman-
ship I assured him I always shot emus in the neck, it saved
damaging the body. For the moment he believed me, then,
with a bright look, asked me how many emus I had shot. I
had to admit—only one.

That afternoon we cooked the emu, at least Moanya and
Jabiaba cooked it, while Lauri and I took photographs, and

made notes, for the preparation and cooking were most carefully carried out, and in a way we had not seen before.

The distribution of the emu, being governed by strict
rules, similar to those of the distribution of the kangaroo,
left me, the hunter, with very little meat. As I was con-
sidered to be a single man, my wife not being with me, my
share of the emu was half the skin—which, to European
teeth and jaws, was as inedible as sponge rubber—the ribs
and the neck, which had no meat on them worth mentioning,
the liver and the heart. The legs and the lower half of the
body, most of the meat, went to the other people. The
position was serious, so I said to Jabiaba:

'S'pose my *minma* (wife) bin here, how much meat she
get?'

'Him get one *tjundu* (leg),' said the old man.

'Very well,' I replied. 'S'pose this time we bin gammon
(pretend) she camp longa me.'

Jabiaba saw the point, and passed over the leg.

On the return journey we spent more time than was
necessary looking for water; not that we were in any danger,
but because we were anxious to avoid a second visit to Piltadi.
Our food stocks were low, and Piltadi meant an additional
two days before we could reach the supplies at Oparinna.

Late one afternoon both Tjundaga and Moanya suggested
we should visit Kuna rock-hole, for it was a very 'big' water,
and never went dry. Although, by then, Lauri and I were
doubtful about any 'big' water, there was nothing else to do
but take the men's advice; so, off we went.

Their estimate was better than on previous occasions, for
Kuna held about forty gallons of black stagnant water,
sufficient to give the camels a few buckets apiece, and
replenish our canteens. When the camels smelt the water
they started to cry. But as they had only been without a
drink for a little over three days, and therefore were not
desperately in need, I told Tjundaga not to unload the
beasts; we would take water to them. But Tjundaga, tired,
and a little recalcitrant, slipped the loads from their backs.
One by one the great creatures rose to their feet, and walked

towards our precious water. We tried to head them off, but they continued on their way as if we were not there. I threw sand in their faces, hit them across the head with branches, and, as a last futile resort, when one of them bent down to drink I struck it across the nose with my pith topee. Though the blow made not the slightest difference to the intentions of the camel, it made all the difference to my topee—it was wrecked beyond repair; perhaps, after all, a fitting end to an old servant.

Regardless of anything we could do, short of killing, those camels continued to drink, even, as if in derision, licking the surface of the rock until not a drop remained. Never have I disliked the supercilious air of a camel so much as I did that evening. Still, all's well that ends well. We found plenty of water late next afternoon, and our troubles were over.

Although the uncertainty about water was our greatest care, there were many irritating pests that had to be endured, foremost among them being the prickles. Nature seemed to have excelled herself in creating sharp-spined herbage and trees. Every leaf of the dead finish tree has a point as fine as a needle; spinifex is a continual torture to beasts and man; the buckbush sheds its thorns in millions; and the goat-head breaks into seed-cases with points so sharp that I have even found them sticking in my finger nails. On the plains, on the hillsides, the prickles abound in countless numbers. We found them everywhere; on the camel saddles, in the sleeping-bags, and even in the most out-of-the-way parts of our clothing.

Many times during the day the aborigines walked to the side of the track to take prickles from their feet, or sat down, sharpened a twig, and dug out an offending thorn from their rubber-like soles. Nor were the dogs exempt, for every now and again one of them would bite at its foot to remove a prickle.

Though we became more or less philosophical about those pests, the sharp twinge of pain which accompanied an unexpected contact with one, especially when we were tired, called forth words which, I am afraid, would not be acceptable in polite society.

For the last month I had walked through those prickles and over the rough, stony hillsides in thin-soled rubber shoes, first my own and then Lauri's, two sizes smaller, holes cut out for the big toes, and split down the middle so that my feet could get into them. Walking in those shoes was most uncomfortable, for they neither gave protection from the multitudinous prickles, nor support to the feet among the rough boulders. Yet, in spite of their disadvantages, those shoes were a boon, for without them I could not have climbed over the ranges to gather the details of the legendary places.

When first I had to use sandshoes, all my leather boots having worn out, my feet ached almost to the limit of my endurance, but towards the end of our stay in the Mann Ranges I found I was having much less trouble. Without knowing it, the necessity of having to protect my feet against the jagged rocks and uneven surfaces had made me adopt the aboriginal way of walking, which I had admired at Katatjuta some months earlier; that is, the choosing of a good foothold for every step. Unconsciously, pain had taught me what every aboriginal learns in childhood, how to walk with the least damage to my feet.

CHAPTER XXII

The Culture of the Desert Aborigines

NOTHING WHATEVER HAD altered at Oparinna. Our tents stood isolated on the black, dusty flood-plain, and Nibiana's camp, cluttered with camel saddles, boxes and gear, seemed to have as many aborigines sitting round it as it had when we left a month previously. Except a goanna skin which some hungry dog had eaten, nothing had been touched, not even the goods or the food in the tents. That was no surprise to me, because I knew from some years of experience how honest the native people were, although when first I learned of that honesty it came as a surprise.

On that occasion I was a member of an anthropological expedition to the eastern deserts of Western Australia, and was among aborigines who, up to that time, were practically untouched by a white civilization. In the early days of our stay we had made some attempts to guard our supplies against theft. But as time went on, and we became more and more interested in the people, we became less and less concerned about our goods, until toward the end no one troubled to look after the camp at all. There were open bags of flour, cases of dried fruit, boiled sweets, and tobacco lying in full view of the native people, yet, though we were absent from the camp for hours on end, so far as we knew nothing whatever was stolen.

On returning to civilization, I talked a great deal about the honesty of those aboriginal folk. Some of my hearers were polite, some sceptical, and others, more vocal, said:

'That might be true of the wild blackfellows, but wait until you get among the civilized ones; they'll steal the very holes out of your socks.'

Within two years I was among the civilized aborigines, people who had been in contact with our culture for over fifty years. Yet, though I pitched my tent in a creek-bed out of sight of the European buildings, was absent many hours during the day, and every night, and in that tent were supplies of tobacco, food and sweets, again nothing was taken.

From that time onward, when among the natives, I have never guarded my goods, and the story has always been the same.

I was aware that the aborigines stole from some white folk, and not from others, and had often wondered why, until some native men in the western Macdonnell Ranges told me about the ill-treatment they had received at the hands of a certain station owner. Knowing that the aborigines had speared some of that man's cattle, I said to them:

'Yes, I know he's been cruel to you, but why do you steal his cattle? You don't steal from the missionary or from myself.'

'That's different,' they explained. 'We spear that man's cattle because he beats us, and takes our women from us; but we don't steal from the missionary or yourself, because you don't do those things.'

After all, that attitude of mind was thoroughly logical, for the law of reciprocal punishment is as much a part of the code of aboriginal behaviour as is the law of reciprocal giving. It can be taken as an axiom that, where the aborigines have any choice of action, the measure of the white man's treatment of them can be judged by their treatment of him.

With that experience behind me I had no fear of what would happen to our goods at Oparinna, even though, when we left, there were about twenty natives round the spring, and every one of them, with the exception of Nibiana, had had to hunt for a livelihood. Yet within those two tents, tied with no more than cotton tapes, were ample supplies of food and tobacco. Numidi had not even taken her dress, much as she tried to coax it out of me previously.

As soon as I straightened out the tent, I called the lady across and passed her back the much-coveted frock. She took it from me with a bright smile, saying as she slipped the ragged, filthy thing over her shoulders:

'I thought Tjamu bin want to take *raga* (dress) back to his own *minma* (wife); but s'pose his *minma* got big mob.'

To see Numidi before and after I gave her that dress, was to see a slim, lovely body suddenly change into a ragged scare-crow; and the same change takes place when a native man dons the cast-off garments of a European.

Some people insist on clothing aboriginal men and women, because, they contend, it is respectable, though in doing so they too often sign their death warrant; for whereas after a heavy rain the skin of a native is dry in about three minutes, it will not be dry in three days if he is wearing a sack coat, and longer if he is unfortunate enough to possess an old overcoat. As the desert people have no waterproof shelters, no knowledge of the danger of wet clothes, and little or no immunity from pulmonary diseases, they die in alarming numbers from tuberculosis and allied diseases; and so is respectability satisfied!

It seems to me the purist often becomes an impurist towards the nakedness of the aborignes. Day after day I had watched the beautiful, unclothed bodies of the men as they strode alongside us. They were a continuous delight to the eye, their skin shining with health, their rippling muscles, and their regal carriage. The older aboriginal men, especially, impressed me with their natural dignity, a dignity which is the outcome of the structure of their society. In an aboriginal community, there are no social grades among the men of the same age. There are no patricians and com-moners, no rich and poor, no leaders and followers; nor are there any chiefs to oppress and rob the people, for there is no organized warfare, therefore no armies to lead. The responsibilities, as well as the powers of government, are in the hands of the experienced, well-informed old men. It is small wonder, then, that the elders should possess a mental poise, and a balance, which belongs only to the best in our own civilization.

Our investigations had shown us that not only the social qualities, but also the intelligence, of the desert aborigines was of no mean order. There has been, and indeed still is, an erroneous belief that the intellectual capacity of a society may be estimated by the number of tools it possesses; that is,

THE LEGEND OF THE PLEIADES

(a) "The marks of the encounter are there today, the place where one of the women had seated herself . . . ," *(Page 156.)*

(b) ". . . a hole dug by one of them in the search for food. Lying beside that hole is a block of stone, the transformed carrying dish . . . ." *(Page 156.)*

THE LEGEND OF THE SPIRIT CHILDREN

(a) "Those infants are now boulders; two of them, egg-shaped, contain an inexhaustible supply of health spirit children, the little, silvery-haired Yulanya." *(Page 158.)*

(b) "The other boulders, similar in shape, but more irregular in outline, are the source of all the mis-shapen babies." *(Page 158.)*

by the simplicity, or otherwise, of its material culture. The Australian aboriginal has, in general, a remarkably limited culture; no permanent homes, no metal tools, no pottery, no bow and arrow, no agriculture, and only the simplest of hunting equipment.

On that account many writers have described him in the most derogatory of terms, 'little more than beasts,' 'the lowest type of humanity,' 'scarcely human,' terms which, unfortunately, have led to a poor regard of the native people.

The fact that our companions, with their five simple tools—the men, a spear and spear-thrower; the women, carrying-dishes, grinding-stones and a digging-stick—are able to live in an arid desert, in which the white man dies unless he takes his food with him, is surely an indication of, at least, a normal level of intelligence. Actually the desert people, whose life is one of continuous movement, have learned what we have not: how to get along with a minimum of equipment. They are entirely mobile. Should a family decide to go on a journey, the man will pick up his hunting weapons, the woman put her carrying-dish on her head, take her digging-stick in her hand, and, whether absent for days, weeks or months, the family have all they need to gain a livelihood.

There is no doubt that the Pitjendadjara tribe has the most limited material culture of any living people; even their stone tools, and their method of making their wooden implements, take us back to man's earliest times. The study of the evolution of tools reveals an increasing simplicity in form and a crudity of finish in the stone implements of ancient peoples, even among the indigenous inhabitants of Australia. Starting from the finely finished leaf-shaped spear points of north-western Australia, the tools of the aborigines can be traced through progressively simpler types, until we come to the chipped pebbles found in some of the old camp sites, tools which possess but a minimum of flaking to give them a cutting edge. It had been assumed that there must have been a time in the history of man when he did not flake his tools at all, but used the sharp corners of pieces of rock to bruise or cut the wood into shape. But no one expected there would be living in the world today men who were practising so simple a technique.

Yet we saw Jabiaba and his companions manufacture a wooden spear-thrower, employing, except for the final smoothing, crude unflaked stones that they had picked up from the hillside. One stone, weighing about seven pounds, was used to cut and split the primary slab from the living mulga tree, an operation that took over an hour of continuous labour. Smaller, sharp-edged stones, about the size of one's fist, were then utilized in the long, tedious task of removing the dense heart-wood, and shaping the implement. Jabiaba finished the tool by smoothing it with the adze-stone, mounted in the end of his spear-thrower. He fitted a throwing peg at one end of the implement and a mass of spinifex gum, in which he embedded a fragment of fine-grained quartzite for cutting, at the other. The making of the spear-thrower involved about four hours of continuous work.[1]

The spear-thrower of the desert people has several uses. As a spear-thrower, it is an extended arm by which the weapon can be thrown further; as a cutting tool, it serves a multitude of uses; as a dish, the hollow body is utilized to contain food; and for fire-making the thin edge of the spear-thrower is rubbed across a split log until the heat from the friction lights the powdered wood-dust.

The spear is a simple shaft, about nine feet long, made from several lengths of tecoma vine, bound together with kangaroo sinews. There is a hardwood blade at one end, fitted with a wooden barb, and a shallow hole at the other to accommodate the peg of the spear-thrower.

The wooden dishes of the women, chopped with unflaked stones from a hollow bole on the trunk of a gum tree, entails, for their making, three to four days of continuous labour. The dish, like the spear-thrower, has a wide range of uses: as a baby's cradle, as a food and water container, and as a hold-all, in which the grinding-stones and other

[1] See Mountford, C. P., 1941 *Transactions Royal Society of South Australia,* Vol. 65 (2), pp. 312-316, for full description.

(a) ". . . it was a common sight to see one of the young girls with a half-grown dog held across her back in the same manner as the older women carry their babies." *(Page 173.)*

(b) ". . . the women, with carrying dishes, grinding stones and a digging stick, are able to live in an arid desert." *(Page 169.)*

"The dish . . . has a wide range of uses; as a baby's cradle; . . . ."   *(Page 170.)*

small articles are carried when the women are on food-gathering journeys. Their digging-stick is a straight branch of mulga, sharpened to a chisel point in the fire; and their grinding-stones, a flat slab and a round boulder.

Although food - gathering is monotonous, and often arduous, the work is communal, for the women always travel together. The experiences of those food-gathering journeys form a never-failing source of conversation, and the almost exclusive subject in their drawings, as Lauri found out, for he had been concentrating on the art of the women.

The women used to get as much fun out of producing the drawings as Nibiana did from acting as Lauri's interpreter, for Nibiana, in her simple way, had become most attached to my young companion, and enjoyed every opportunity that came her way to help him. One evening at Oparinna, when I had left my tent for a breath of fresh air, I looked towards Lauri's tent, to see it simply bulging with people. I went across to find out what was going on, and there, in the light of two candles—for, like almost everything else, the petrol lamps had ceased to function—Nibiana and Lauri were crouched over a crayon drawing. I think every woman in the camp was in that tent, either bending over my companion or telling Nibiana, in unison, the meaning of the designs in the drawings. From all that babel of tongues, poor Nibiana was trying to sort out the relevant details to pass on to Lauri. Every now and again she would lose patience and shout out irritably:

'*Wonga wia* (talk none, or shut up), me and Lauri no more bin hear, s'pose too many fella bin talk together.'

Even the camp dogs were trying to force their way among the feet and legs of the women, for the aboriginal's dog is happiest when closest to its human companions. I had been impressed by the close companionship between the aboriginal and his dog. The creature lives as much in the life of the family as do the children; it sits round the same tiny fire, and at night lies close to the man or the woman. I had often seen Jabiaba asleep with his dog on his arm. Even the

N

newly born baby at Ernabella had to share the fire with the
dog belonging to the mother.

An aboriginal seldom hits his dog, though when a white
man demands that the dogs be kept away from his camp—
they usually come to steal—the position is different; then
the aborigines, ever courteous to those they accept, will chase
the dogs away. But the dogs suffer so little punishment at
the hands of their masters that it was difficult to make them
leave our camp when they came on entirely peaceful errands.
Several times, when writing up my diary late at night, I felt
something creep up against me, and on looking down saw
some poor scarecrow of a dog, which had made the mistake
of thinking I was one of the brown people. I would give
the dog a push, and, in my best European manner, yell 'Get
out,' something that would have made a dog belonging to
a white man shrink and run. But not so with the aboriginal's
dog; it simply did not know what the noise meant, and, when
I pushed it away, it looked at me in a puzzled manner, and
crept back to its old position.

Although there is a bond of affection between the
aboriginal and his dog, the latter is almost always half
starved. The aborigines, able only to gather enough to keep
themselves, and sometimes hard set to do even that, leave
their dogs to fend for themselves, as we found to our cost,
when, with great cunning, they raided our supplies. At
Ernabella some dogs had pulled a small bag of flour from
the stack, torn it open and had a meal. I went across to the
camp and made a fuss about the theft; but every woman
assured me it was someone else's, not her dog, which had
stolen my food. Yet, sitting round those women's fires were
the dogs, carrying their guilt with them, for each had some
of the tell-tale flour stuck to its wet nose.

There was general indignation in the camp one evening at
Oparinna when a visitor brought in the news that baits, laid
by the missionary, had poisoned a number of aboriginal dogs.
That information revived the thought of grief which always
followed the visits of trespassing doggers, who shot the dogs
of the natives in order to collect the Government bounty

paid for dog scalps. Moanya also told us of a time when some of his family, being short of food on a long journey, decided to kill one of their own dogs; but after having done so, they were so sorry that they could not eat it, and mourned all night over the body, just as though it were a human being.

The native women also take a great interest in the litters of pups, and often carry them from camp to camp in their wooden dishes; and it is quite a common sight to see one of the young girls with a half-grown dog held across her back, in the same manner as the older women carry their babies.

An aboriginal child, before he is old enough to walk all day by himself, is a heavy load for his mother, so Lauri and I, to give some over-burdened mother a rest, often put a little chap on the saddle in the front of us. During the last day on the journey between Oparinna and Erliwunyawunya, a pregnant mother had passed her boy of about eighteen months of age up to me. Though the riding must have been most uncomfortable, he sat astride the saddle for about an hour before he showed any signs of weariness, his chubby little hands holding tightly to the iron frame-work. Even then, it was not until the sun had set that the little fellow called out. Straightway his mother, who had been close beside the camel all the time, took off her rag of a dress, for me to wrap around her son. I carried him in my arms until we stopped, some two hours later, and did not hear another whimper; yet he must have been cold in that inadequate covering. I was, in my thick clothing.

We spent a most uncomfortable night at Erliwunyawunya. A roaring gale blew from all quarters. Several times during the night Lauri and I arranged our beds for a wind coming from one direction, only to find, when we climbed into them, that the wind had changed, and was blowing dust and ashes in our faces. The camp gear was everywhere; the wind-breaks were over the top of us, and in the morning our ears and nostrils were almost blocked with dust. We were pleased, in more ways than one, to mount the camels and set out on the last stage to Ernabella.

CHAPTER XXIII

We Return Home

As THE CAMELS PLODDED their way along the track that took us back to our own civilization, my mind was occupied with thoughts of the simple, courteous folk we were leaving behind: quizzical, humorous Jabiaba, quick-tongued Numidi, kindly Nibiana, and sterling, dependable men like Moanya, Tjundaga and Tjalerina.

It had been a memorable experience to have been able to see, if only for a short time, and then but imperfectly, the functioning of one of the most primitive cultures of mankind, a culture with tools so simple that the gaining of a livelihood in the desert environment is a remarkable achievement, a culture with a code of laws so well balanced that the people are at peace with each other, and in harmony with their surroundings. Nor were the aborigines living crudely or brutishly, as many would have us believe, but following a way of life rich in philosophical thought, in cultural expressions and communal living.

The philosophies of the aboriginal people link them closely to their environment; they are not, like ourselves, 'lords of the creation,' but a part of creation itself. The great 'Dream Time' progenitors of the animals, the birds and the plants, are also the progenitors of the people; the same *kuranita* which vitalizes all living things also provides the aborigines with vitality. The natives are an integral part of the life around them, no greater and no less than any of its components.

The cultural expressions of the people, in story, song and drama, are indissolubly linked with the exploits of, and the beliefs associated with, those great mythical forebears. Although those expressions are primitive, and limited in scope, they are of prime importance in the tribal pattern, the vital media through which are kept alive the beliefs of the tribe, and the codes of behaviour of the daily round.

Just as the links of the aborigines with their past are strong and enduring, so is their relationship and their control of the world round them. It is the aborigines, by their increase ceremonies, who cause the animals to reproduce, the trees to blossom and bear fruit, and the grasses to bring forth seed. Because they are responsible for the creation of life, the aborigines do not destroy it beyond their immediate requirements. They are too much within the orbit of nature to understand, much less to get pleasure from, useless killing. So that, although the brown men have lived in the desert country for unknown generations, nowhere, away from the settlement of white man, is there any evidence of destruction by human beings; no hillsides stripped of trees, no flats turned into dust bowls, nor are the creatures exterminated.

The close identification of man with his environment also governs the ownership of aboriginal land. The tribal boundaries of each family were determined by their semi-human forebears, who not only created the natural features of the country, the rocks, trees and streams, but also the myths, songs and ceremonies which belong to those natural features. It would be impossible, therefore, for a family of Kangaroo-men to possess the tribal lands of, say, the Emu-men. True, the Kangaroo-men might even drive the Emu-men from the country, and roam over it at will, but as they would not know the associated myths and ceremonies the land would still belong to the Emu-men, no matter what the Kangaroo-men might do.

The relationship of the aborigines to each other is as well balanced as their relationship to their land. From that relationship has developed a fully co-operative society, based on a system of reciprocal giving and receiving that reaches out to every aspect of life, social intercourse, ceremonial procedure, and the gathering and distribution of food.

It was in their food-sharing that we saw the co-operative system most clearly at work. No doubt the frequent shortages of food made some equitable system of distribution a necessity; nevertheless, such a system could only function smoothly in a disciplined society, where the laws are fully accepted, and the spirit of fair play is predominant.

As well as being co-operative, the social culture of the desert people appears to be non-competitive. We found no evidence of one trying to excel the other; no talk of one group being the more skilful or efficient; in fact, even among the children, we did not see a competitive game.

It might seem, on superficial observation, that the dividing of the tribe into two social groups, the *taminiltjan* and the *nanunduraka,* would have led to competition and consequent inter-group conflict. But that possibility was countered by the law of exogamy, which demands that everyone must marry outside his own group. As every member of the tribe, therefore, is related to a number of persons in the other half of the tribe, to some of whom he will owe special obligations, the community is so interlocked with relationships, responsibilities and privileges, that group conflict is impossible.

So, as there is no evidence of competition between either group or individuals—always a fruitful source of discord, no condition where one feasts and another starves, no private ownership of land, and no social grades, it follows that there is no need of organized warfare, with its attendant bloodshed and misery. There will be, naturally, potential lawbreakers, and individual quarrels, for they will occur in any community; but, as the pressure of ridicule and public disapproval is usually a sufficient deterrent to keep them within bounds of the tribal pattern, it is seldom that physical punishment is required.

The smooth working of the aboriginal society is further strengthened by the stability of its laws, customs and conditions, a stability established by the usages of generations of people. The desert aborigines do not have to face—or at least did not until our arrival—the continuous adjustments and disorganization of changing laws. The environment was always the same, the laws were always the same, therefore the way of life remained the same.

It is a remarkable culture, the culture of those desert aborigines; simple, peaceful, co-operative and kindly; free from avarice, bitterness and strife that characterize the more complex civilizations.

But all those things have their price. Although the social conditions of the desert aborigines are almost Utopian in conception and operation, the physical conditions are strenuous, harsh and full of privation. The desert is a hard taskmaster, and life within its boundaries is a difficult life. Long, tiring journeys in the blazing heat of summer, or in the cold of winter, are looked upon as a matter of course; food and water are often scarce; and hunger is a part of the daily round. For those in their prime, the hardships are not excessive; it is upon the children, the pregnant and the aged that the burden falls most heavily. But those hardships and privations are the common lot of the aborigines, the pattern of their existence, patiently and stoically endured. The desert people are a happy people, as devoid of comforts as they are of cares.

Toward the end of the second day we reached Ernabella. Mrs. Ward, with her consistent kindliness, invited Lauri and me to a meal and a bath. We sat round the table for a while talking about our experiences, then returned to camp and to bed.

The strain of the long journey was over; the night was still, and the stars shone like diamonds through the leaves of the trees under which I was camped. Relaxed, at peace with the world, and enjoying the feeling of again being clean, I sank into one of the most refreshing sleeps I had had for a long time.

I awoke at dawn to hear a rooster crowing, then the whinny of a horse. Later came the other sounds of our civilization, the bleating of sheep and goats, someone pumping water, and the white folk moving about.

Those sounds were most pleasant to hear; they were a part of my cultural heritage; they belonged to the association of a life-time. They were to me what the sight of glaciers and green valleys are to a homecoming Swiss, or the roar of London traffic is to a Cockney. They told me I had come home.

Index

Brown, Prior, Anderson Pty. Ltd., Melbourne

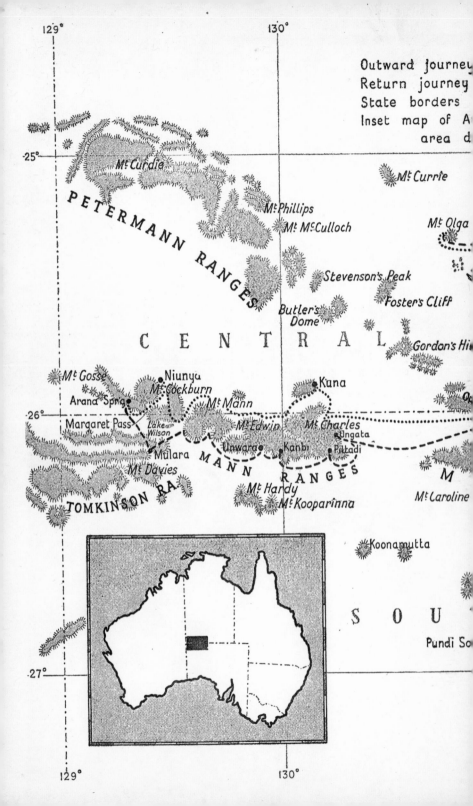